Masters: Art Quilts, Vol. 2

CAROLYN CRUMP ■ JAN MYERS-NEWBURY ■
KARIN FRANZEN ■ EMILY RICHARDSON
■ ANNA TORMA ■ CHUNGHIE LEE ■
GENEVIÈVE ATTINGER ■ MIRJAM PET-JACOBS
■ PAMELA FITZSIMONS ■ PAULA NADELSTERN ■
DIRKJE VAN DER HORST-BEETSMA ■ ROSALIE DACE
■ LESLIE GABRIËLSE ■ NELDA WARKENTIN ■
GAYLE FRAAS AND DUNCAN SLADE ■ DIANNE FIRTH
■ REIKO NAGANUMA ■ SHULAMIT LISS ■ ALICE BEASLEY ■

BEATRICE LANTER ■ TAFI BROWN ■ RISË NAGIN
■ BENTE VOLD KLAUSEN ■ JANE DUNNEWOLD ■
LAURA WASILOWSKI ■ ARTURO ALONZO SANDOVAL
■ IZABELLA BAYKOVA ■ DANIELA DANCELLI ■
MARGERY GOODALL ■ LINDA MACDONALD
■ FENELLA DAVIES ■ RACHEL BRUMER ■
MARYLINE COLLIOUD-ROBERT ■ JIM SMOOTE
■ ELEANOR MCCAIN ■ PATRICIA MALARCHER ■ MISIK KIM ■
ELIZABETH BUSCH ■ DOROTHY CALDWELL ■ TIM HARDING

Masters: Art Quilts, Vol. 2

Major Works by Leading Artists

Curated by Martha Sielman

An Imprint of Sterling Publishing Co., Inc.
New York

WWW.LARKCRAFTS.COM

SENIOR EDITOR
Ray Hemachandra

EDITOR
Julie Hale

ART DIRECTOR
Kay Holmes Stafford

COVER DESIGNER
Meagan Shirlen

CURATOR
Martha Sielman

COVER, LEFT TO RIGHT
Karin Franzen
Bathed in a Turquoise Sky, 2010

Tim Harding
Koi #12, 2000

Izabella Baykova
The Tower, 2008

BACK COVER
Carolyn Crump
Playing the Blues, 2008

SPINE
Leslie Gabriëlse
Woman with Two Gents, 2001

Library of Congress Cataloging-in-Publication Data

Sielman, Martha.
  Masters : art quilts , volume two / curated by Martha Sielman; senior editor; Ray Hemachandra -- 1st ed.
      p. cm.
  Includes index.
  ISBN-13: 978-1-60059-599-8 (PB-trade pbk. : alk. paper)
  1. Art quilts--United States--History--20th century. 2. Artquilts--United States--History--21st century.
I. Title.
  NK9112.S52 2008
  746.460973--dc22
                                        2007031080

10 9 8 7 6 5 4 3 2 1

First Edition

Published by Lark Crafts
An Imprint of Sterling Publishing Co., Inc.
387 Park Avenue South, New York, NY 10016

Text © 2011, Lark Crafts, an Imprint of Sterling Publishing Co., Inc.
Photography © 2011, Artist/Photographer

Distributed in Canada by Sterling Publishing,
c/o Canadian Manda Group, 165 Dufferin Street
Toronto, Ontario, Canada M6K 3H6

Distributed in the United Kingdom by GMC Distribution Services,
Castle Place, 166 High Street, Lewes, East Sussex, England BN7 1XU

Distributed in Australia by Capricorn Link (Australia) Pty Ltd.,
P.O. Box 704, Windsor, NSW 2756 Australia

If you have questions or comments about this book, please contact:
Lark Crafts
67 Broadway
Asheville, NC 28801
828-253-0467

Manufactured in China

ISBN 13: 978-1-60059-599-8

For information about custom editions, special sales, and premium and corporate purchases, please contact the Sterling Special Sales Department at 800-805-5489 or specialsales@sterlingpub.com.

For information about desk and examination copies available to college and university professors, requests must be submitted to academic@larkbooks.com. Our complete policy can be found at www.larkcrafts.com.

Contents

Introduction

What a joy it has been to write this book! It serves as a wonderful complement to *Masters: Art Quilts, Volume 1* and exposes readers to even more groundbreaking work.

During the year I spent conducting research for this project, I made some fascinating discoveries about today's master quilt artists. I tried to be concise and to the point in my essays about these quilters, focusing on the creative techniques they use and what inspires them. But so many of these artists have led such interesting lives that I've decided to use this space to expand on some of their stories.

Take Rachel Brumer, for example. Not only was she a professional modern dancer, she also served as a sign-language interpreter and did a stint in the Ringling Bros. and Barnum & Bailey Circus. In addition to her art quilts, Brumer creates sculptural pieces. Drawing on her experiences as a performer, both her quilts and sculptures explore complex themes about the nature of time.

Alaskan Karin Franzen also has a fascinating personal history. In college she earned a degree in biology and minored in art. She then studied civil engineering. She eventually founded a company that manufactured dog-mushing equipment. Now biology and art both play important roles in her quilts, beautifully detailed compositions that depict birds in the Alaskan wilderness. Franzen's civil-engineering background also influences her work, as she addresses the structural challenges of piecing and display.

Then there's Leslie Gabriëlse. His family was living on the Indonesian island of Java when the Japanese invaded in 1942. Leslie was three when he and his family were placed in internment camps, and painful separations from his parents followed, both during and after the Second World War. Today, Gabriëlse makes striking portraits out of fabric—chic, modern renderings of men and women, some of them life-size. Yet Gabriëlse's subjects often seem pensive and distant, removed from one another—a mood that may reflect the upheaval of his childhood.

Sometimes the artists' stories involve my own breakthroughs concerning their work. As I studied the quilts of Izabella Baykova, I was puzzled by the fact that several of her works feature realistic landscapes paired with abstract geometric shapes that run along one side of the main composition. Were those shapes trial pieces or color swatches? I wasn't sure. Then one morning I saw a watercolor portrait of John Henry by illustrator

Jerry Pinkney in *The Horn Book Magazine*. Pinkney used a similar technique—small brushstrokes of color laid alongside the main figure. And I suddenly understood that, through similar methods, both quilter and painter had focused my attention on their artistry. The strips on the side of the portrait conveyed that I wasn't looking at John Henry. I was looking at a *painting* of John Henry. Likewise, Baykova's swatches of fabric communicate that the viewer isn't looking at a Russian landscape but at an artist's depiction of that landscape. Both works speak not only of an illustrated subject but also of the ways in which the illusion of realism is achieved.

Baykova's shimmering landscapes and crisply depicted folktales are the embodiments of magical realism. Other artists employ realism for very different purposes and often with a twist to convey humor or a definite point of view. Linda MacDonald's slightly surreal compositions of humans and animals communicate her keen political sensibility and concern for the environment. A storyteller at heart, Laura Wasilowski presents offbeat re-imaginings of the material world in colorful quilts that commemorate the joys of everyday life.

Other artists, like Misik Kim and Chunghie Lee, blend the personal and the historical to create quilts with important ties to the past. Kim reinterprets traditional Korean *chogak po* patchwork in quilts that experiment with block size, color, and mood. Lee draws on the design of the customary Korean *pojagi*, or wrapping cloth, as she plays with the concepts of translucency and wrapping. Both artists bring a modern sensibility to time-honored textile practices.

The art-quilt masters in this remarkable collection are men and women of different generations and backgrounds with a wide range of ideas, inspirations, and stories. Each brings a unique personal legacy and perspective to bear on his or her work. Yet all are building on tradition to take the revered craft of quilting into a new era.

I hope you find the artwork included in this volume as fascinating, engaging, and intriguing as I do. Look carefully as you make your way through the book and meander among the quilts, and you'll discover many stories that enrich your appreciation of both art and the world around you.

— Martha Sielman, curator

Carolyn Crump

A FIFTH-GENERATION QUILTER who has also studied painting and graphic design, Carolyn Crump draws on a variety of mediums to create vivid, richly textured portraits and scenes. Like block prints or linocuts, her figures are outlined in black against boldly colored backgrounds. Lively and dynamic, the black lines of each figure create a sense of movement that Crump echoes in images like flowing scarves, billowing ribbons, and flags.

To create a portrait, Crump makes at least 10 different sketches of her subject's face. She then translates her final sketch into a pen-and-ink drawing, which she refers to when selecting the batik and hand-dyed fabrics she favors. She fills her backgrounds with waves of deep, rich color that she punctuates with squares and rectangles.

Crump's expert thread-painting lines blend her appliquéd fabrics together and emphasize the textural nature of her quilts. Her recent pieces combine painting on fabric with appliquéd sections, many of which are created as separate quilted elements and combined to add a three-dimensional aspect to the work.

Consistently powerful, Crump's quilts and the figures they depict offer viewers a window into other worlds—and a deep sense of connection to them.

▲ **Cherished Times** | 2007

38 x 34 inches (96.5 x 86.4 cm)

Cotton; appliquéd, machine sewn

Photos by artist

▲ **African Attitude** | 2009

19 x 17 inches (48.2 x 43.2 cm)
Cotton; painted, machine sewn

Photos by Ash Wilson

The Kiss | 2009 ▶

14½ x 10 inches (36.8 x 25.4 cm)
Cotton, silk; appliquéd,
machine sewn

Photo by Ash Wilson

◀ **Awakening Spring** | 2007

52½ x 34 inches (1.3 x 0.8 cm)
Cotton, glass beads; appliquéd,
machine sewn, hand sewn

Photos by Rodolfo Hernandez

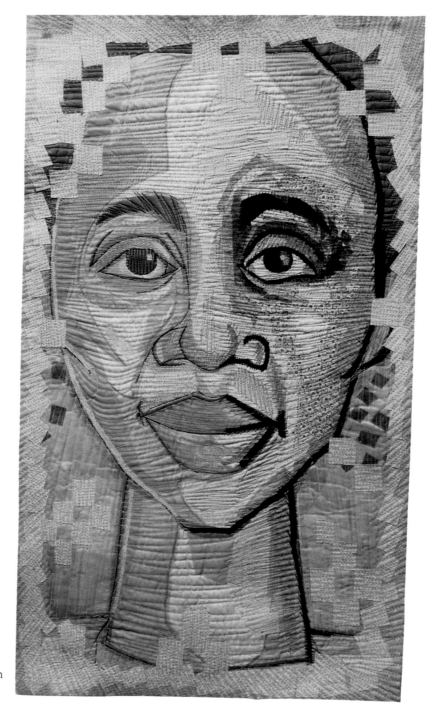

" I like challenging myself to be better. When I fail at one process, I don't stop until I find a solution. **"**

Dichotomy | 2009 ▶
31 x 18 inches (78.7 x 45.7 cm)
Cotton; appliquéd, machine sewn
Photo by Ash Wilson

" The medium of fiber draws me into a world of unlimited imagination. "

◀ **Wings of Faith** | 2008

28 x 26 inches (71.1 x 66 cm)
Cotton; appliquéd, machine sewn

Photos by Rick Stein

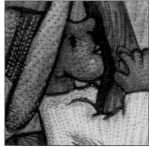

Like Father, Like Son | 2009 ▶

26 x 16 inches (66 x 40.6 cm)
Cotton, paint; appliquéd,
machine sewn

Photos by Ash Wilson

◀ **Dusky Cove** | 2007

38 x 53 inches (0.9 x 1.3 m)
Cotton; appliquéd, machine sewn

Photo by Ash Wilson

Spirit of Rita | 2006 ▶

40½ x 54 inches (1 x 1.4 m)
Cotton; buttons, appliquéd,
machine sewn

Photo by Rick Gardner

" Quilting
gives me the
opportunity to
express what
I imagine, to
materialize it
on a surface for
others to see. "

◀ Playing the Blues | 2008
14 x 10 inches (35.6 x 25.4 cm)
Cotton; appliquéd,
machine sewn
Photo by Ash Wilson

Jan Myers-Newbury

INSPIRED BY THE COLORS SHE IS ABLE TO CREATE in her dye baths, Jan Myers-Newbury uses a variation of Japanese arashi shibori to produce the seductive hues that make her quilts glow. During the arashi shibori process, Myers-Newbury wraps white fabric around a pole and lashes it with string or thread, then submerges it in a series of dye baths. The wrapping and tying result in thin lines of color that enliven the surfaces of her quilts.

Myers-Newbury begins each new quilt by playing with fabric on her design wall, and color dictates nearly all of her creative decisions. She cuts her fabric into squares and rectangles, then arranges and rearranges the shapes until they coalesce into an ordered whole.

Piecing the components together smoothly—taming the colors into strict geometric relationships—is the part of the quilting process that Myers-Newbury enjoys most. She follows the shibori lines and linear elements with machine-quilted lines, taking care that she doesn't intrude on the primacy of the color interactions. The results are works of luminous beauty that offer refuge from the chaos and disorder of daily life.

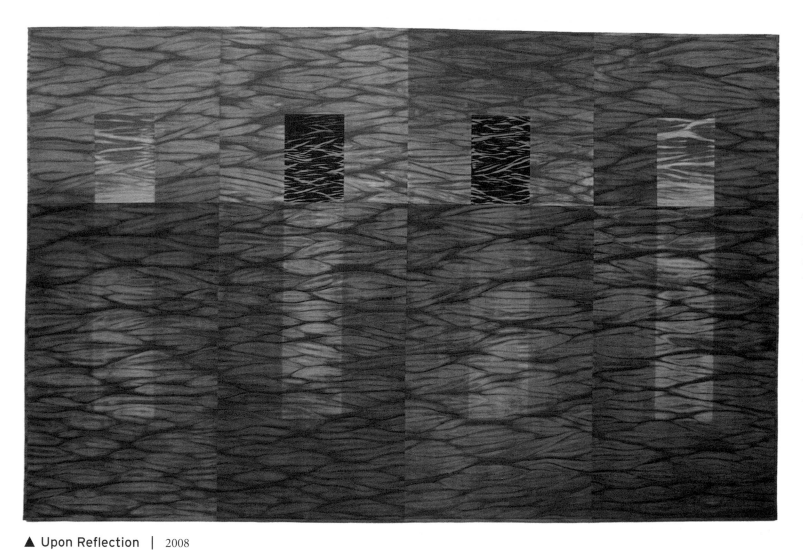

▲ Upon Reflection | 2008

48½ x 75 inches (1.2 x 1.9 m)
Cotton; hand dyed, discharged, arashi shibori,
damp resist, machine pieced, machine quilted

Photos by artist

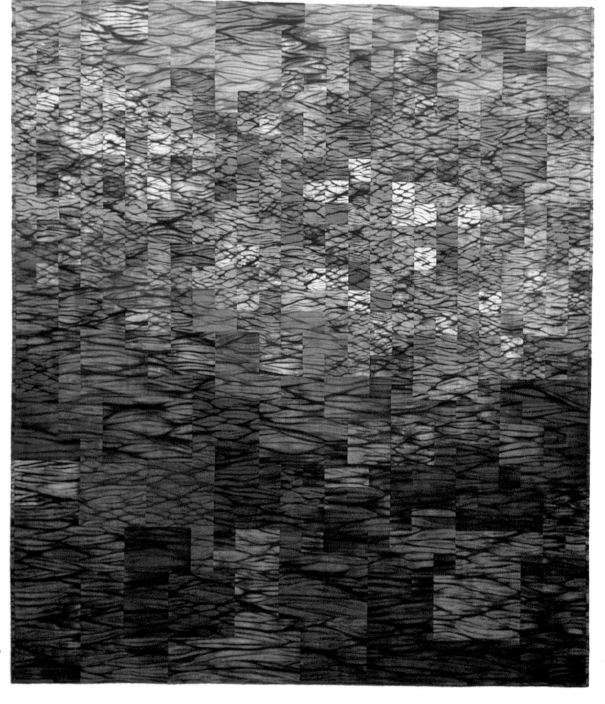

" I never have a
notion of how a
finished piece will
look at the outset.
I start with fabrics
that I like and
arrange them by
color and scale.
Once I see how
things are filling
in, I start to work
more specifically to
balance the whole. "

Urubamba | 2006 ▶
62 x 52½ inches (1.5 x 1.3 m)
Cotton; hand dyed, arashi shibori,
machine pieced, machine quilted
Photo by Sam Newbury

▲ **Wild Thing** | 2008

    63 x 84 inches (1.6 x 2.1 m)
    Cotton; hand dyed, arashi shibori, discharged,
    machine pieced, machine quilted
    Photo by Sam Newbury

" In 1992, I made my
first all-shibori quilt.
Since then, I've been
working mostly
with arashi shibori,
combined at times
with clamp resist. "

Coronae | 2004

59 x 42 inches (1.5 x 1 m)
Cotton; hand dyed, arashi shibori,
damp resist, machine pieced,
machine quilted
Photo by Sam Newbury

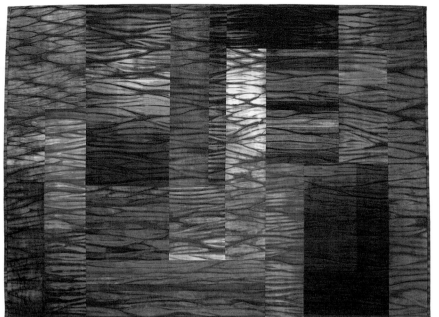

Boogie Woogie | 2005 ▶

33 x 44 inches (83.8 x 111.8 cm)
Cotton; hand dyed, arashi shibori,
machine pieced, machine quilted

Photos by Sam Newbury

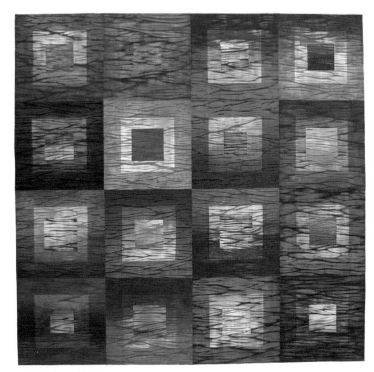

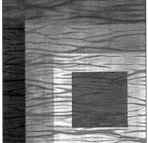

◀ **Ode to Albers** | 2004

75 x 75 inches (1.9 x 1.9 m)
Cotton; hand dyed, arashi shibori, damp resist,
machine pieced, machine quilted

Photos by Sam Newbury

▲ It's Dark Outside | 2006

64 x 54 inches (1.6 x 1.3 m)
Cotton; hand dyed, arashi shibori,
machine pieced, machine quilted
Photo by Sam Newbury

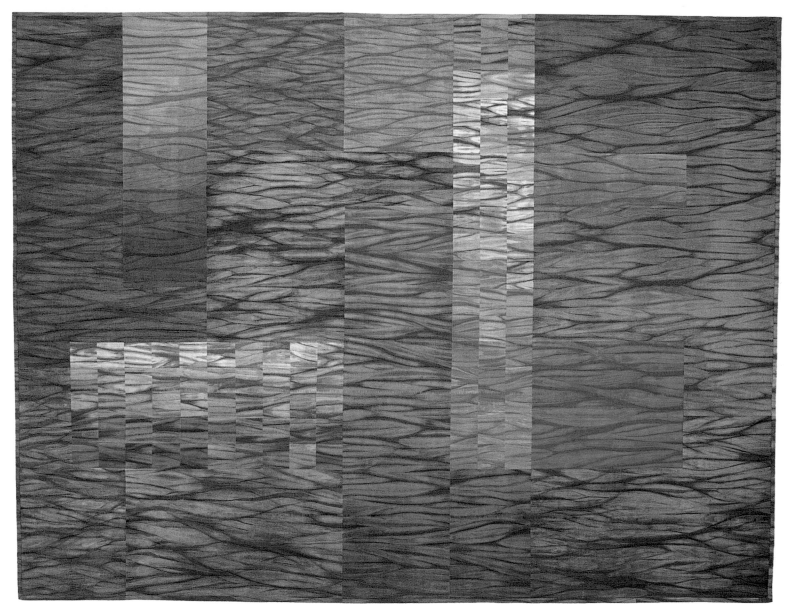

▲ Interruptions | 2008

    34 x 44 inches (86.4 x 111.8 cm)
Cotton; hand dyed, arashi shibori,
machine pieced, machine quilted

Photo by Sam Newbury

" My work has always been about intellectual and spiritual matters.

It's important to me that a quilt be beautiful and orderly. "

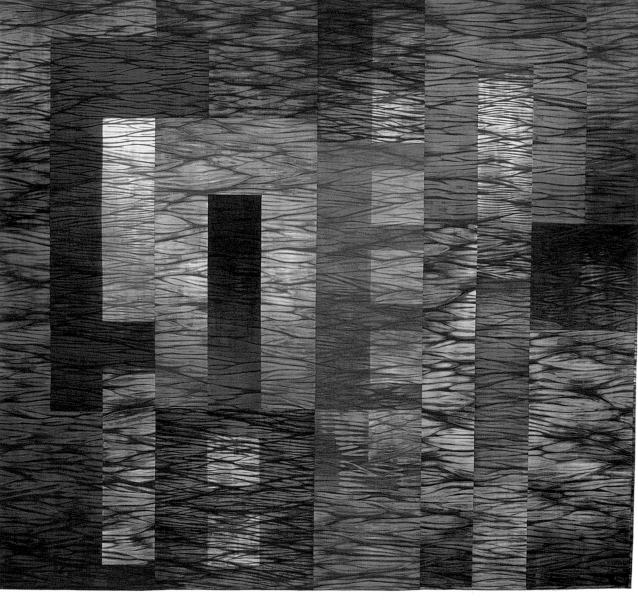

▲ Moog | 2006

68 x 72 inches (1.7 x 1.8 m)
Cotton; hand dyed, arashi shibori,
damp resist, machine pieced, machine quilted

Photo by Sam Newbury

▲ Ten Squared | 2009

60 x 60 inches (1.5 x 1.5 m)
Cotton; hand dyed, discharged, arashi shibori,
machine pieced, machine quilted

Photo by artist

Karin Franzen

ENDURING ALASKA'S LONG WINTER SEASON, Karin Franzen finds endless inspiration in her wild surroundings. Her quilts feature detailed renderings of plants and wildlife that are intricately configured in raw-edge appliqué from scraps of recycled clothing. In order to offset the literal nature of her depictions, Franzen adds layered sheers to each piece to communicate a sense of nature's mystery.

Many of Franzen's early pieces feature the typical quilt form, with a front, a batting, and a back. Recent works—quilts made of multiple sheer layers that can be viewed from both sides, and finished pieces mounted on wooden frames—reflect her experiments with different types of presentation. Franzen is also interested in how air currents can change the way a quilt is viewed, as its layers shift and change in the light.

She uses machine quilting to highlight foliage, tree trunks, and water ripples and to create a variety of abstract spirals and zigzags. Her backgrounds are pieced or built up from multiple layers of silk organza, which she dyes, discharges, and screen-prints. She fills each piece with detail, which draws viewers in.

Graceful and majestic, Franzen's cranes and ravens serve as reminders of nature's fragility.

▲ Pirouette IV | 2007

49 x 42 inches (124.5 x 106.7 cm)
Silk organza over cotton, wool, linen, acetate, polyester, rayon thread, oil sticks, fabric paint, bleach; low-water immersion dyed, screen-printed, discharged, raw-edge appliquéd, machine pieced and quilted
Photos by Patrick Endres

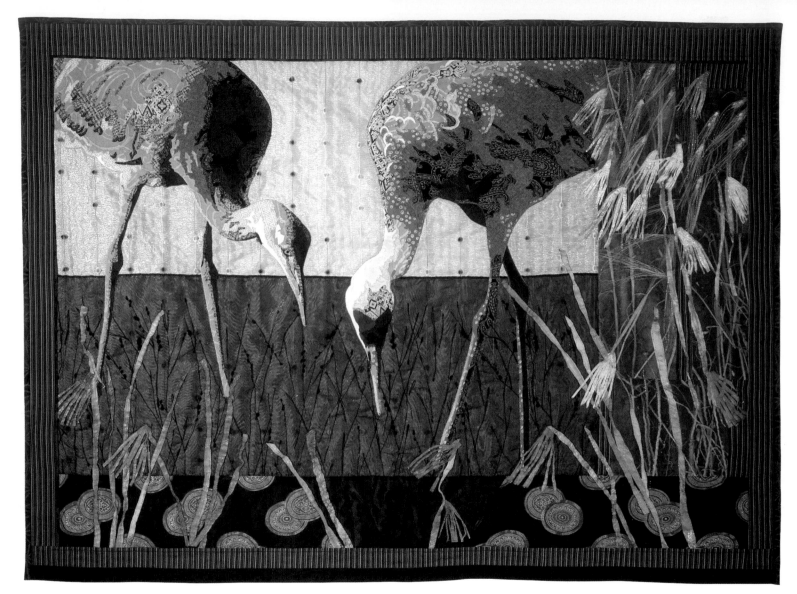

▲ **The Barley Eaters** | 2007

35 x 48 inches (88.9 x 121.9 cm)
Used clothing, synthetic sheers, Tyvek, acrylic paint,
cotton batting and backing, rayon thread, photographs; machine quilted, pieced, raw-edge appliquéd,
photo transfer

Photo by James Barker

Pirouette III | 2007 ▶

49 x 42 inches (124.5 x 106.7 cm)
Cotton batting, silk organza,
cotton, wool, linen, acetate, rayon
quilting thread; dyed, discharged,
overdyed, screen-printed,
raw-edge appliquéd, machine
pieced and quilted

Photos by Patrick Endres

❝ As much as possible, I construct my pieces from used clothing. Recycling is fundamental to the

tradition of quilting, and I consider it my one true reference to the customary form. ❞

KARIN FRANZEN

▲ Fibonacci's Crane: Stretching | 2007

24 x 36 inches (60.9 x 91.4 cm)
Cotton, silk, rayon; machine pieced and
quilted, hand embroidered, screen-printed,
raw-edge appliquéd

Photo by James Barker

" The visual interaction of light with sheers and the tactile qualities
of various textiles provide me with endless inspiration. "

The Raven Clan | 2009 ▶

69 x 41 inches (1.7 x 1 m)
Silk organza, cotton, wool, linen, rayon,
polyester, silk, cotton batting, rayon thread,
cotton thread; low-water immersion dyed,
screen-printed, raw-edge appliquéd,
machine pieced and quilted

Photos by Patrick Endres

KARIN FRANZEN

◀ **A Time to Dance: April 28th** | 2008

47 x 44 inches (119.4 x 111.8 cm)
Silk organza, synthetic sheers, wool, silk, linen, rayon,
polyester, acetate, cotton, rayon thread, cotton thread,
fabric paint; low-water immersion dyed, silk-screened,
discharged, raw-edge appliquéd, machine quilted,
hand stitched

Photos by Eric Nancarrow

A Time to Dance: September 9th | 2008 ▶

48 x 55 inches (1.2 x 1.4 m)
Silk organza, synthetic sheers, wool, silk, linen,
rayon, polyester, acetate, cotton, rayon thread,
cotton thread, fabric paint; low-water
immersion dyed, silk-screened, discharged,
raw-edge appliquéd, machine quilted,
hand stitched

Photo by Eric Nancarrow

A Time to Dance: May 17th | 2008 ▶

60 x 43 inches (1.5 x 1.1 m)
Silk organza, synthetic sheers, wool,
silk, linen, rayon, polyester, acetate, cotton,
rayon thread, cotton thread, fabric paint;
low-water immersion dyed, silk-screened,
discharged, raw-edge appliquéd, machine
quilted, hand stitched

Photos by Eric Nancarrow

▲ **A Time to Dance: June 21st** | 2008

49 x 45 inches (1.2 x 1.1 m)
Silk organza, synthetic sheers, wool, silk, linen, rayon, polyester, acetate, cotton,
rayon thread, cotton thread, fabric paint; low-water immersion dyed, silk-screened,
discharged, raw-edge appliquéd, machine quilted, hand stitched

Photo by Eric Nancarrow

" I have a deep love
for experimentation
that springs from
my fascination
with fabric. **"**

Bathed in a Turquoise Sky | 2010 ▶

69½ x 41 inches (1.7 x 1 m)
Silk organza, cotton, wool, linen, polyester,
rayon, thread, synthetic sheers; low-water
immersion dyed, screen-printed,
machine pieced, raw-edge appliquéd,
machine quilted

Photos by Patrick Endres

KARIN FRANZEN

Emily Richardson

EXPERIENCE IN FASHION DESIGN and theatrical costuming gives Emily Richardson a unique appreciation for color and texture—two elements that characterize her ethereal quilts. Working spontaneously, Richardson typically begins each quilt with pieces of sheer silk organza, which she paints with thin washes of acrylic, letting the paint run and pool. Richardson then cuts up the pieces and arranges them on her design wall, rearranging and layering the fabric until a cohesive composition emerges. The buildup of sheer layers serves to deepen colors, define lines, or mask what lies beneath.

Using single strands of embroidery floss that are matched to each piece, Richardson hand sews the layers together with an overcast stitch. She works with 20 to 30 needles at a time, so that she doesn't have to stop to re-thread. Her palette often reflects what she sees around her. A trip to Japan resulted in a series of works filled with clear pinks, lilacs, and cerulean blues.

The world provides plenty of inspiration for Richardson, but she says that the key to making art lies in not knowing what she's going to create next. Dense with form and color yet airy and light, her quilts seem like visions from another world.

▲ **Until the Day** | 2008

    44 x 42 inches (111.8 x 106.7 cm)

    Silk, acrylic paint; hand sewn

    Photos by Rick Fine

Quick Water | 1998 ▶

41 x 28 inches (104.1 x 71.1 cm)
Silk, cotton, netting, acrylic paint;
hand sewn

Photo by Rick Fine

" My goal is to create
a visual image that
has never existed—
not even in
my imagination. "

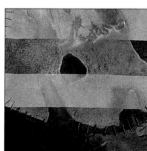

◀ **After the Sea Ship** | 2007
44 x 34 inches (111.8 x 86.4 cm)
Silk, acrylic paint; hand sewn
Photos by Rick Fine

" I chose my medium because of the range of possibilities offered by the materials and techniques. From the fluid act of painting on cloth to the working of stitches, I'm continually excited by what I see. "

EMILY **RICHARDSON**

Masque of Oriana | 2004 ▶
72 x 48 inches (1.8 x 1.2 m)
Silk, acrylic paint, cotton;
hand sewn
Photo by Rick Fine

▲ **Cloud Forest** | 1999

42 x 56 inches (1 x 1.4 m)
Silk, acrylic paint; hand sewn
Photo by Rick Fine

▲ Goblin's Progress: In the Air | 2006

25 x 25 inches (63.5 x 63.5 cm)
Silk, cotton, acrylic paint; hand sewn

Photo by Rick Fine

Undertow | 2006 ▶

69 x 48 inches (1.7 x 1.2 m)
Silk, acrylic paint; hand sewn

Photos by Rick Fine

" Sometimes I'll compose an entire piece on the wall, pinning bits of painted fabric in place, then dismantling the whole to start afresh. This gets me fully acquainted with the parts of a quilt. "

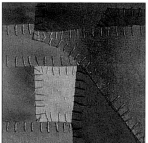

◀ **Came out of the Sea** | 2003
51 x 29 inches (129.5 x 73.7 cm)
Silk, acrylic paint; hand sewn
Photos by Rick Fine

EMILY **RICHARDSON**

Full Fathom Five | 2001 ▶

60 x 31 inches (1.5 x 0.7 m)
Silk, linen, acrylic paint;
hand sewn

Photo by Rick Fine

▲ **Blossoms of the Waves** | 2006

28 x 44 inches (71.1 x 111.8 cm)
Silk, cotton, acrylic paint; hand sewn

Photo by Rick Fine

Anna Torma

REDWORK EMBROIDERY, A TECHNIQUE used to create stitched line drawings in red thread on muslin fabric, first became popular in the late 1800s. Anna Torma modernizes this traditional practice in her visually complex work. Drawing on her diaries, pictures made by her children, and the traditional decorative motifs of her native Hungary, Torma brings to her quilts a complex abundance of imagery, including flowers, monsters, and birds.

Over the years, Torma has refined the vocabulary of symbols that she now uses as a private code in her visual storytelling. She achieves breathtaking cascades of color and form by thread painting on backgrounds that are collaged from found vintage textiles and covered with rows of stitching. The level of skill involved in her embroidery contrasts with the childlike nature of her figures.

In her complex work, Torma explores concepts of femininity, domesticity, and ethnicity, and she also asks viewers to create their own stories: Are those figures hunting? Is sexuality monstrous? Are the roses to be admired, or should they be removed before they completely choke the garden?

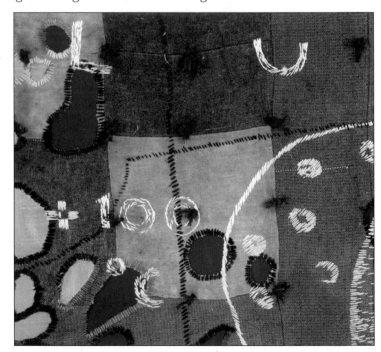

▲ Soldier's Quilt I | 2009

$80^{15}/_{16}$ x $57^{3}/_{4}$ inches (2 x 1.4 m)
Found military uniforms, women's silk shirts, drawings;
hand sewn, hand restored, hand embroidered

Drawings by Istvan Zsako
Photos by artist

◀ Rondo | 2006
72¹¹⁄₁₆ x 53⅛ inches (1.8 x 1.3 m)
Found objects, digital print,
commercial fabrics;
hand stitched
Photo by artist

▲ Jardin du Wiltz I | 2006

62½ x 51³⁄₁₆ inches (1.5 x 1.3 m)
Cotton, linen; hand embroidered,
hand quilted

Photo by Natalie Matutschovsky

" My recent work is influenced by primitive, outsider, and children's art—by their expressive directness and ability to communicate to a wide range of viewers. **"**

Soldier's Quilt II | 2009 ▶

78⁹⁄₁₆ x 64¹³⁄₁₆ inches (2 x 1.6 m)
Military uniforms, found
embroidery; silk appliquéd,
hand stitched

Photo by Istvan Zsako

" My approach to new work is usually instinctive instead of predetermined.

Imagery and structure come first, while decisions about technique are secondary. *"*

▲ **Draw Me a Monster** | 2004

59 x 54 inches (1.5 x 1.3 m)
Cotton, linen, cotton thread;
hand embroidered, reverse appliquéd

Photo by Natalie Matutschovsky

▲ Paper Dolls | 2008

    57 x 57 inches (1.4 x 1.4 m)

    Commercial fabrics, cotton, found embroidery; hand embroidered, hand stitched

    Photo by artist

◀ **Red Flowers I** | 2006

66 x 52⅜ inches (1.6 x 1.3 m)
Cotton, silk; appliquéd,
hand embroidered,
hand quilted

Photo by David Zsako

▲ Metamorphosis | 2008

72¹¹⁄₁₆ x 78⁹⁄₁₆ inches (1.8 x 2 m)
Linen base, found textiles, commercial fabrics,
silk threads; hand embroidered, hand stitched

Photo by artist

" I use hand embroidery as a special tool when I need to 'draw' on a piece. If I want the image I'm creating to resemble a painting, the embroidery stitches will be dense and play a main role. "

▲ **Draw Me a Garden** | 2006

62½ x 52¾ inches (1.5 x 1.3 m)
Cotton, commercial fabrics;
hand embroidered, hand stitched

Photo by artist

ANNA **TORMA**

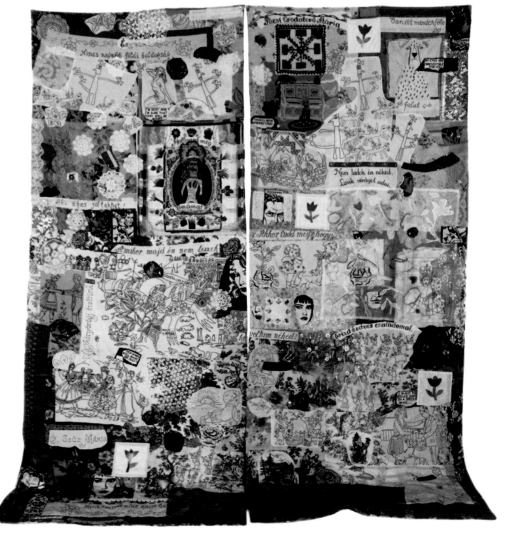

▲ **Critical Mass** | 2009

92⁵⁄₁₆ x 57 inches (2.3 x 1.4 m)
Found women's needlework, commercial fabrics;
hand embroidered, hand stitched

Photo by David Zsako

Chunghie Lee

FACES PEER OUT AT US from the captivating quilts made by Korean-born artist Chunghie Lee. Inspired by historic Korean women who created *pojagi* (po-jah-ki)—the two-sided wrapping cloth with ties used for carrying items and decorating the home—Lee sometimes includes their photographs in her quilts. Drawing on the design of these traditional textiles, Lee has taken the *pojagi* concepts of patchwork, translucency, and wrapping in many different directions over the years. She has produced quilts designed for display on the wall, wearable art pieces that enfold the body, and room-size installations that wrap an entire space.

To make her *pojagi*, Lee transfers antique photos, natural bamboo leaves, and Korean biblical proverbs onto silks, paper, or hemp cloth before hand piecing irregularly shaped patches together.

Her pieces are often multi-colored and embroidered in a traditional fashion with flowers and other nature motifs. Lee works with translucent fabrics that make it possible for hand-sewn, rolled, or flat-fell seams to serve as integral design elements. The translucent layers shift with the light, so that the colors change according to the viewer's perspective.

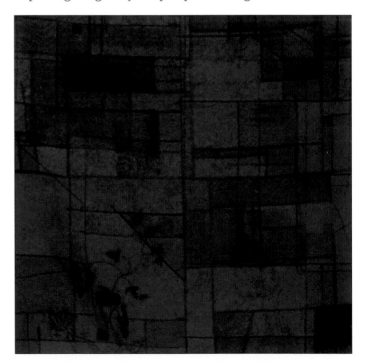

In her installations, Lee often includes a grid marked with stones along with her fiber pieces. The stones are metaphors for the hand stitches used in making *pojagi*, a tradition in which small elements slowly accumulate to form a larger, greater whole.

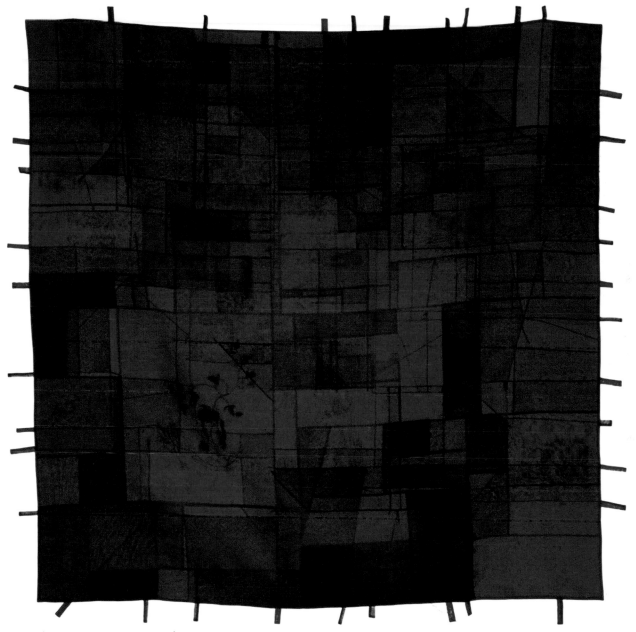

▲ No-Name Women | 2005
43⁵/₁₆ x 43⁵/₁₆ inches (110 x 110 cm)
Silk, photo images; silk-screened, machine sewn
Photos by Hongik Photo Art

▲ Pojagi and Beyond; Installation at Heyri | 2003

Middle piece: 196½ x 196½ inches (5 x 5 m)

Hemp; machine sewn

Photo by artist

▲ No-Name Women Installation | 2006
Ivory piece: 169 x 11¹³/₁₆ inches (4.3 x 0.3 m)
Red piece: 145 x 98 inches (3.7 x 2.5 m)
Hemp, photo images; hand dyed,
silk-screened, machine sewn
Photo by Jiyoung Chung

" I view patchwork
as a metaphor
for life: As
individuals, we
may feel isolated
and alone,
but in reality
I think we're
part of a larger
composition that
has harmony
and meaning. **"**

◀ **No-Name Women** | 2009

23⅝ x 23⅝ inches (60 x 60 cm)
Silk; machine sewn

Photo by artist

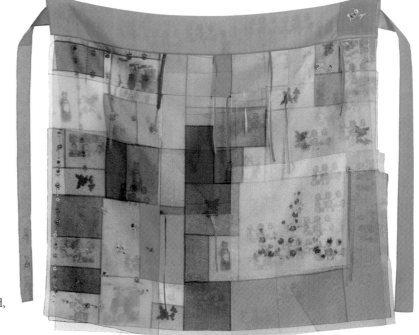

No-Name Women | 2002 ▶

51¹/₁₆ x 70¾ inches (1.3 x 1.8 m)
Silk, photo images; hand embroidered,
silk-screened, machine sewn

Photo by artist

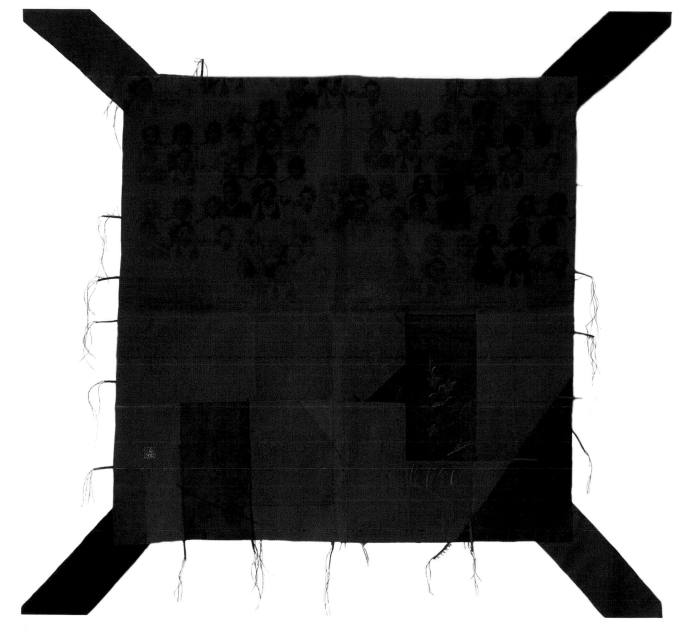

▲ No-Name Women Pojagi | 2004

60 x 60 inches (1.5 x 1.5 m)
Silk, photo images; silk-screened,
machine sewn

Photo by Hongik Photo Art

▲ No-Name Women | 2004

47⅛ x 94⁵⁄₁₆ inches (1.2 x 2.4 m)
Paper, photo images, hemp; hand dyed,
silk-screened, machine sewn

Photo by Hongik Photo Art

No-Name Women Installation | 2005 ▶

145⅜ x 98¼ inches (3.7 x 2.5 m)
Silk, hemp, photo image; hand dyed,
silk-screened, machine sewn

Photo by Jiyoung Chung

" The women
who made pojagi
many generations
ago are a great
inspiration to
me. They had no
social position or
independence, yet
they endured. "

◀ No-Name Women Bamboo Scrolls | 2006

Each scroll: 177 x 26 inches (4.5 x 0.6 m)
Indigo hemp; hand dyed, silk-screened,
machine sewn

Photo by Hongik Photo Art

" In the 1990s, when I began to make pojagi, I started going to the market to buy traditional Korean textiles. That's when I first discovered the beauty of my own culture's fabrics. It was like finding treasure in my own backyard. "

▲ No-Name Women | 2009

$23^5\!/_8$ x $23^5\!/_8$ inches (60 x 60 cm)
Silk; machine sewn

Photo by artist

▲ No-Name Women Paper Pojagi | 2008
23⅝ x 23⅝ inches (60 x 60 cm)
Paper, photo images; silk-screened
Photos by artist

▲ Reverse Side

Geneviève Attinger

HUMAN RELATIONSHIPS OFTEN ALTERNATE between the passion of union and the pain of separation. Geneviève Attinger's artwork presents both the passion and the pain from a woman's perspective. Working with a wide variety of fabrics found in French flea markets or salvaged from decorator discards, Attinger uses free-motion machine stitching to create portraits that she traps behind a variety of barriers, including nets, window curtains, and barbed wire. She bends, twists, and pierces her fabric to create further allusions to the barriers we often create between one another.

Attinger savors the tactile, sensual aspects of fabric and often works with unusual materials such as cheesecloth or burlap because of their texture. Motifs associated with women, such as apples, flowers, and the moon, appear frequently in her quilts.

In her symbolic explorations of themes such as motherhood and politics, Attinger's work depicts the darker, melancholy side of human relations. But some of her pieces are also filled with love, as they reflect upon the ways in which relationships can grow and change over time.

▲ Johanne au Piecing | 2005

34 x 35 inches (86.4 x 88.9 cm)
Cotton, linen; hand dyed, free-motion machine
embroidered, appliquéd, machine sewn

Photos by Cédric Duclos

" My work starts with careful planning. I draw nudes or portraits based on photos and create templates from them that I machine embroider onto appliquéd pieces. I then set the figures in a scene, using textiles to define my narrative. "

◀ La Chemise Fantasmée | 2006
54 x 32 inches (1.4 x 0.8 m)
Cotton, hemp, wire, wood; hand dyed, discharged, free-motion machine embroidered, machine appliquéd and sewn
Photo by artist

▲ Outre-Pudeur | 2006

    41 x 41 inches (104.1 x 104.1 cm)
Cotton, linen, satin, net; hand dyed, discharged, free-motion
machine embroidered, machine appliquéd and sewn

Photo by artist

▲ **M. La Pétrifiante** | 2007

16 inches (40.6 cm) in diameter
Cotton jersey, satin, silk, organza,
metal, rope; hand dyed, free-motion
machine embroidered

Photo by artist

▲ **Eden #1** | 2009

49 x 51 inches (124.5 x 129.5 cm)
Linen, cotton, velvet, satin; hand dyed, discharged, monoprinted,
free-motion machine embroidered, machine and hand sewn

Photo by artist

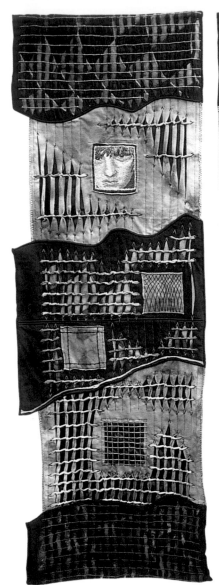
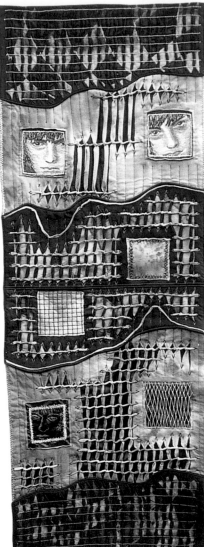
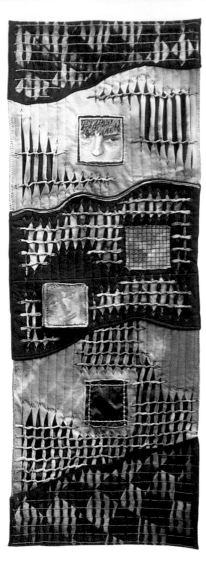

▲ Les Recluses | 2003

58 x 54 inches (1.5 x 1.4 m)
Cotton; hand dyed, solvent transfer,
knotted, free-motion machine
embroidered, hand embroidered,
appliquéd, machine sewn

Photo by artist

" I work freely with my sewing machine, using it as a

pencil to create pieces that blend expression and form. "

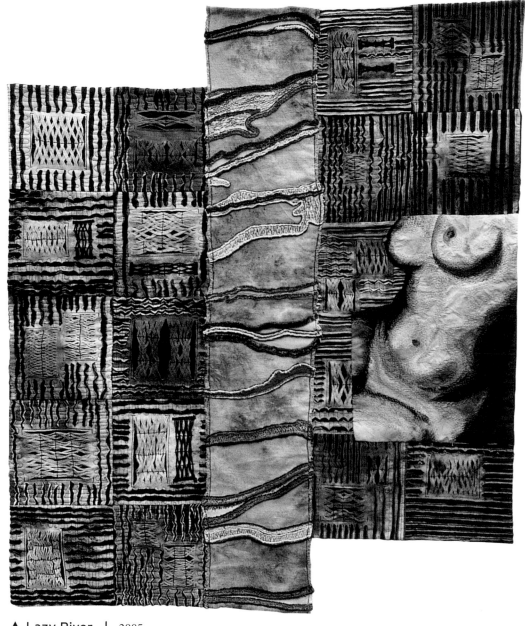

▲ Lazy River | 2005

44 x 37 inches (111.8 x 94 cm)
Cotton, linen; hand dyed, free-motion machine embroidered,
pulled thread work, machine appliquéd and sewn

Photo by Cédric Duclos

GENEVIÈVE ATTINGER

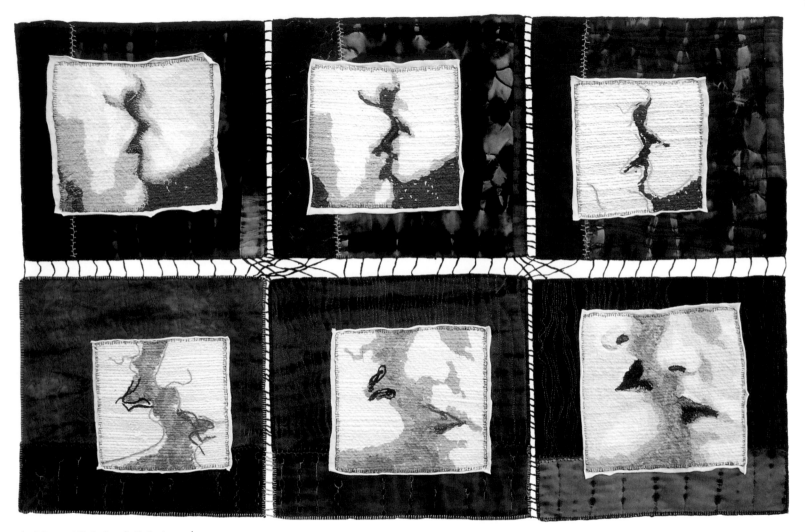

▲ D'une Histoire à l' Autre | 2008

30 x 46 inches (76.2 x 116.8 cm)
Cotton jersey; hand dyed, discharged, free-motion
machine embroidered, hand embroidered

Photo by artist

" My quilts are my words. I use them to tell stories. "

▲ La Traversée des Ruptures | 2005

Each: 8 x 8 inches (20.3 x 20.3 cm)
Cotton, satin, metallic fabric, metallic thread;
free-motion machine embroidered, machine
appliquéd and sewn, knotted

Photos by artist

La Précieuse | 2008 ▶

5 x 5 inches (12.7 x 12.7 cm)
Linen, cotton, metallic fabric;
hand dyed, free-motion machine
embroidered, machine appliquéd
and sewn

Photo by artist

Mirjam Pet-Jacobs

MESSAGES BOTH OBVIOUS AND ELUSIVE permeate the provocative works of Dutch quilter Mirjam Pet-Jacobs. Written in English, many of Pet-Jacobs' communications are literal. Others are hidden, written on tiny scrolls that she wraps up and attaches to her work. Some of her messages are purely visual, conveyed through bands of color splashed across black-and-white photos. Close quilting lines in myriad hues cover the surfaces of her work, creating a wealth of subtle tones and textures.

Pet-Jacobs' quilts often feature what she calls the "Mimi figure"—a long, thin, abstract form that symbolizes the vulnerability and helplessness of humankind. The Mimi figure usually projects an area of calm that contrasts with an emotionally charged, chaotic background.

A frequent experimenter, Pet-Jacobs often works with new forms and recently completed a video installation that includes footage of her quilting, projected through several layers of suspended sheer fabric so that the installation is "stitched" together by light. Her complex, atmospheric quilts resonate with viewers, as they explore the nature of solitude and human connection.

▲ **Mimiquilt IV: Ancestral Shadows** | 2002

53⁹/₁₆ x 49⁵/₈ inches (1.3 x 1.2 m)
Cotton, silk, blends, organza, tulle, metal;
hand painted, reverse embroidered, appliquéd,
stamped, machine sewn, hand sewn
Photos by Peter Braatz

▲ **Mimiquilt VI: Degradation** | 2003

44$\frac{1}{16}$ x 40$\frac{15}{16}$ inches (112 x 104 cm)
Cotton, silk, sheers, polyester, Ultrasuede; hand painted,
stamped, stenciled, appliquéd, machine sewn, hand sewn
Photo by Peter Braatz

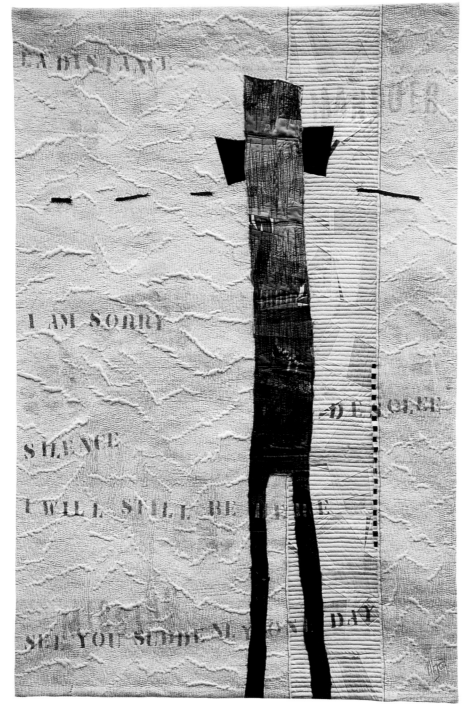

" I view myself
as a visual artist
who works with
textiles, not as a
textile artist. **"**

◀ **The Silence in Between** | 2009
66¹³/₁₆ x 49⁵/₈ inches (1.7 x 1.2 m)
Cotton, silk, silk velour; dyed, painted,
appliquéd, reverse appliquéd,
screen-printed, stamped, stenciled,
machine sewn, hand sewn, rubbed
Photos by artist

" In my work I try to
capture intangible
experiences—
phenomena like
time and sound. "

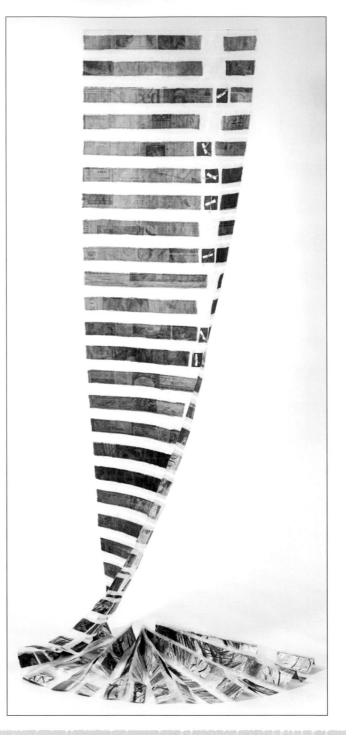

Le Mantra III: Missing Messages | 2009 ▶

163⅞ x 23⅝ inches (4.1 x 0.6 m)
Nonwoven sheers, silk, rope, paper, acrylics, ink,
metal foil; stamped, screen-printed, rolled, tied,
torn, collaged, machine sewn

Photos by Dirk Leemans

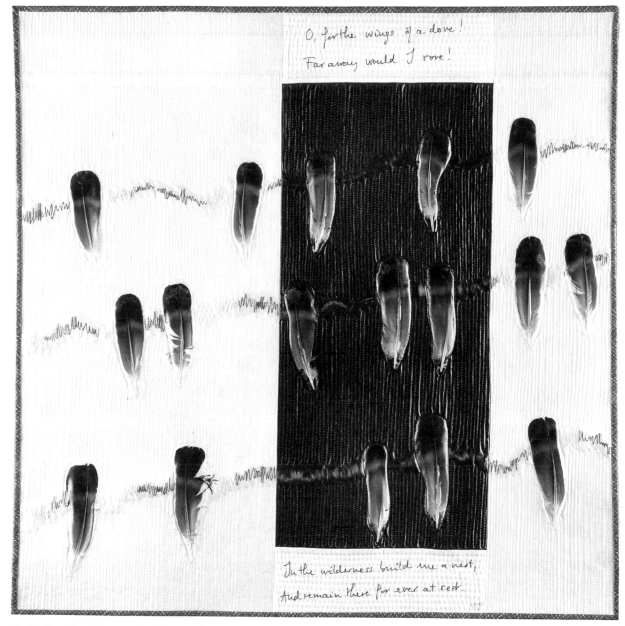

O, for the wings of a dove!
Far away would I rove!

In the wilderness build me a nest,
And remain there for ever at rest.

▲ O, for the Wings of a Dove | 2004

28¾ x 28¾ inches (73 x 73 cm)
Cotton, feathers, vinyl; shibori, computer printed,
embroidered, machine sewn, hand sewn

Photo by Arthur Bagen

" My main inspiration is the world around me. I observe and reflect, peel a moment or a memory down to its core, then rebuild it layer by layer. "

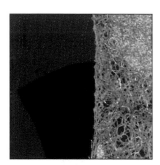

Moments Musicaux | 2008 ▶

68⅜ x 52¾ inches (1.7 x 1.3 m)
Cotton, silk, synthetics; dyed, painted, embroidered, appliquéd, machine sewn, hand sewn
Photos by Dirk Leemans

▲ **Think of the Mothers I: The Preparing** | 2007

38¹⁵/₁₆ x 38¹⁵/₁₆ inches (99 x 99 cm)
Silk, synthetics, cotton, organza; appliquéd,
reverse appliquéd, embroidered, hand dyed, painted,
photo transfer, stamped, machine sewn, hand sewn

Photo by artist

▲ **Think of the Mothers II: The Violence** | 2007

38¹⁵⁄₁₆ x 38⁹⁄₁₆ inches (99 x 98 cm)
Silk, synthetics, cotton, organza; appliquéd, reverse appliquéd,
embroidered, hand dyed, hand painted, photo transfer, stamped,
machine sewn, hand sewn

Photo by artist

▲ **Think of the Mothers III: The Grief** | 2007

39⅜ x 39¾ inches (100 x 101 cm)
Silk, synthetics, cotton, organza; appliquéd, reverse appliquéd,
embroidered, hand dyed, hand painted, photo transfer, stamped,
machine sewn, hand sewn

Photo by artist

Pamela Fitzsimons

CLOTH ACTS AS A METAPHOR for the fragility of the Australian landscape in Pamela Fitzsimons' beautifully crafted, richly textured work. The details of the land—its patterns, colors, and textures, its changing shapes and cycles—are her focus. Fitzsimons lives in New South Wales, a region of ancient sandstone strewn with fossils from the Permian period. Her surroundings have given her a fascination with the concept of time. Fitzsimons' work is also influenced by the possum-skin cloaks and wrapping cloths made by aboriginal women—the earliest Australian patchwork.

She dyes her silks and wools with eucalyptus leaves and bark, sometimes using simple tied resists to create patterns. Her dyed fabrics are roughly torn or cut and then pieced and appliquéd back together. The patterns of her hand quilting marks lend fascinating texture to each work, as the lines of stitching mimic geological layers of sandstone. These lines change direction, create grids, and scrunch the fabric. They create furrows and shadows that cause shifts in the color of the cloth.

Applying slow techniques and painstaking craftsmanship to each of her quilts, Fitzsimons reminds viewers of the importance of time.

▲ Skin/Earth | 2008

33 1/16 x 34 1/4 cm (84 x 87 cm)
Silk, silk thread; plant dyed, machine pieced,
appliquéd, hand stitched

Photos by David Barnes

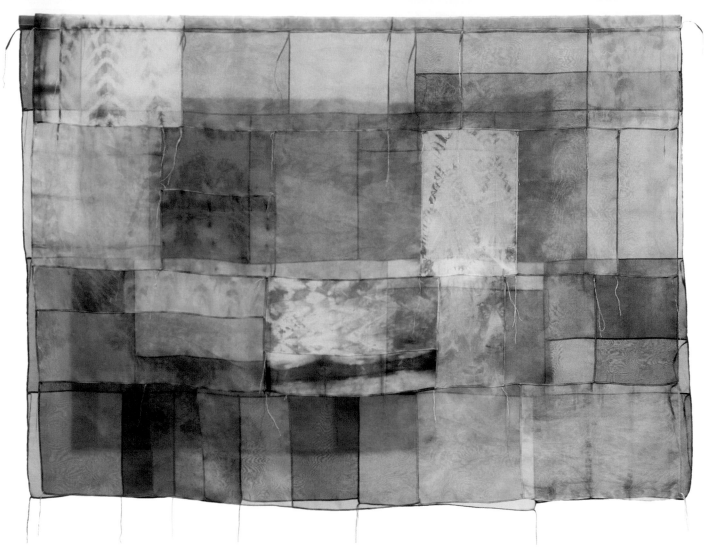

▲ **Extinction Wrap** | 2007
43⁵⁄₁₆ x 59¹⁄₁₆ inches (1.1 x 1.5 m)
Silk, silk and cotton thread; plant dyed,
machine pieced, hand stitched
Photo by David Barnes

" I feel connected to women of past generations
who used needlework as a creative escape and
made do with the materials they had at hand. **"**

▲ **Sandstone Cloak** | 2001

34¼ x 30⁵⁄₁₆ inches (87 x 77 cm)
Silk, wool batting, silk thread; machine pieced,
hand stitched, plant dyed

Photo by Mike Campos

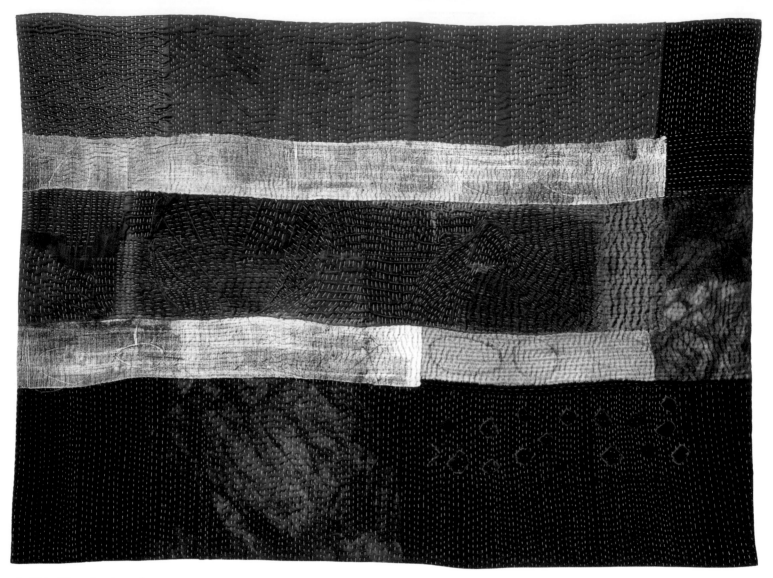

▲ **Skin/Eucalyptus** | 2009

29⅛ x 39¾ inches (74 x 101 cm)
Silk, silk thread; plant dyed,
machine pieced, appliquéd,
hand stitched

Photo by David Barnes

" The methods I employ are simple but time consuming—collecting plant material for dyeing, simmering fabric for hours in a dye bath, and stitching by hand. I enjoy the ritualistic quality of these processes. "

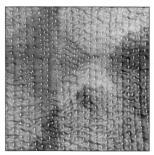

Walking Werekata 2 | 2006 ▶

25⅝ x 27³⁄₁₆ inches (65 x 69 cm)
Silk, silk thread; plant and
rust dyed, machine pieced,
layered, hand stitched

Photos by David Barnes

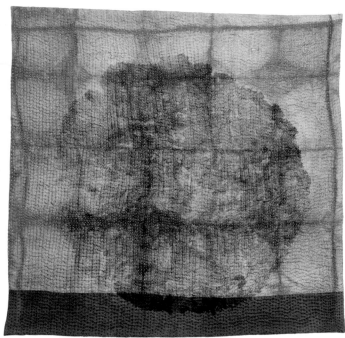

◀ **Fault Line** | 2006

33⅞ x 31⅛ inches (86 x 79 cm)
Wool, silk; plant dyed, machine pieced,
hand stitched

Photos by David Barnes

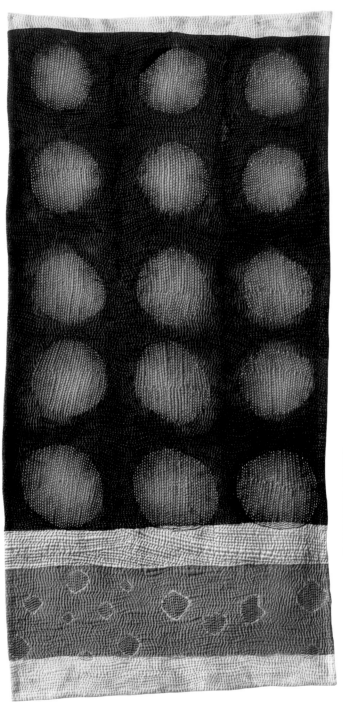

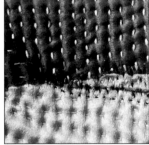

◀ **Fossil Bed #6** | 2004

53¹⁵⁄₁₆ x 29⁹⁄₁₆ inches (1.3 x 0.7 m)
Silk, silk thread; plant dyed,
machine pieced, hand stitched

Photos by David Barnes

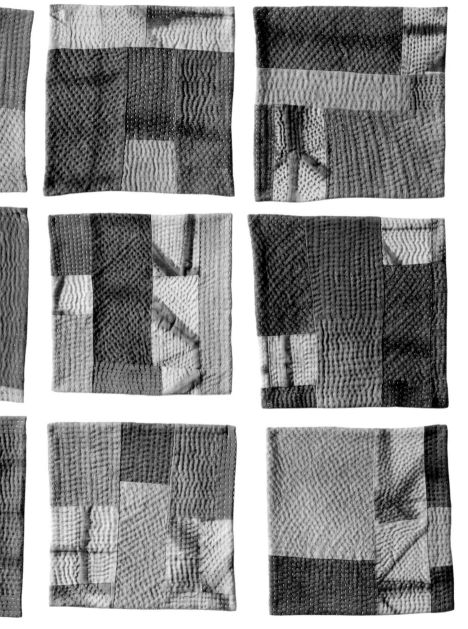

▲ Tessellation Tiles | 2005

Each panel: 9 1/16 x 9 1/16 inches (23 x 23 cm)

Silk, silk thread; plant dyed, machine pieced, hand stitched

Photos by David Barnes

◀ **Werekata 2** | 2005

51³⁄₁₆ x 26³⁄₈ inches (1.3 x 0.6 m)
Silk, silk thread; plant and rust dyed,
machine pieced, layered, hand stitched

Photo by David Barnes

▼ **Rock Fissures** | 2005

30⁵⁄₁₆ x 33½ inches (77 x 85 cm)
Wool, silk and linen thread; plant
dyed, appliquéd, hand stitched

Photo by David Barnes

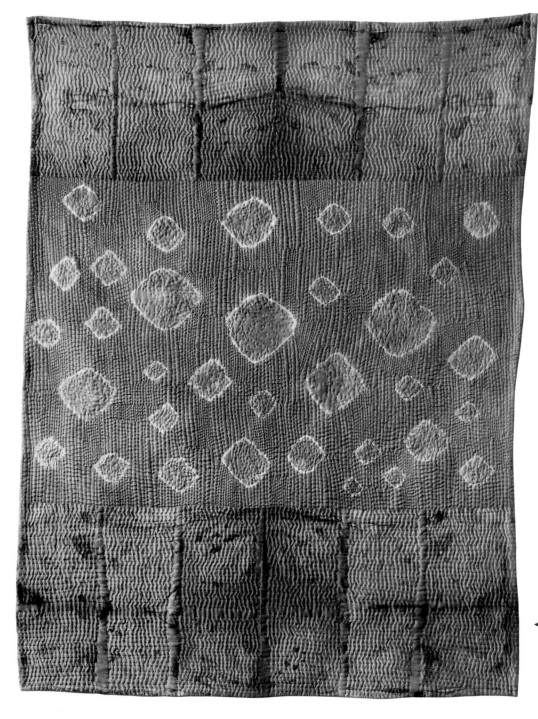

" I view the time
recorded
in the quilting
process as parallel
to the time
imprinted on the
Australian
landscape. "

◄ Fossil Bed #7 | 2005
44½ x 33¹⁄₁₆ inches (113 x 84 cm)
Silk, silk thread; plant dyed,
machine pieced, hand stitched
Photo by David Barnes

Paula Nadelstern

OFFERING THE VISUAL EXCITEMENT of a kaleidoscope through explosions of color and complex, symmetrical designs, Paula Nadelstern's quilts are sumptuously mesmerizing. An avid collector of fabric, Nadelstern has amassed a wide variety of cotton and silk materials, some vintage, some hand dyed, and some commercial with striking symmetrical motifs. Using graph paper and templates, she fussy cuts her fabrics, then machine pieces her forms into triangular wedges that come together to create an illusion of circularity. Nadelstern fools the viewer's eye by camouflaging her seams, a trick that makes it seem as though her images can shift and whirl.

Though the planning of each shape requires precision, Nadelstern adds elements of surprise to her work with her fabric choices and piecing. She works to emulate what she refers to as the "succession of chance interlinkings" found in kaleidoscopes.

Her quilts are like optical illusions, filled with images that seem fleeting and spontaneous. Gorgeously rich and vibrantly colorful, Nadelstern's work is always surprising.

▲ **Kaleidoscopic XXXIII: Shards** | 2007

64 x 57 inches (1.6 x 1.4 m)

Cotton; machine pieced, hand quilted, machine quilted

Photos by Luke Mulks

▲ **Kaleidoscopic XXVII: September 11** | 2002

47 x 42 inches (119.4 x 106.7 cm)
Commercial cottons and silks; machine pieced, machine quilted

Specialty textiles by Lunn Fabrics, Pieces of Eight, Skydyes, and Rebecca Yaffe
Machine quilted by Jeri Riggs
Photo by Karen Bell

" There are two
kinds of surprises:
the meticulously
planned kind
and the happy
coincidence.
Making
kaleidoscope
quilts allows me
to synthesize
elements of both. "

▲ **Kaleidoscopic XXII: Ice Crystals** | 2000
    54 x 41 inches (1.3 x 1 m)
    Cottons, silk; machine pieced, hand quilted
    Photos by Karen Bell

▲ **Kaleidoscopic XXX: Tree Grate, 53rd and 7th** | 2004

51½ x 58½ inches (1.3 x 1.5 m)

Cottons, silk; machine pieced, hand quilted

Photo by Karen Bell

▲ Kaleidoscopic XXXII: My Brooklyn Bridge | 2006

36 x 36 inches (91.4 x 91.4 cm)
Cottons, silk; machine pieced, hand appliquéd, hand couched,
long-arm quilted, hand quilted

Photo by Karen Bell

▲ **Kaleidoscopic XVIII: Chai** | 1998

37 x 37 inches (94 x 94 cm)
Cottons, silks; machine pieced, hand quilted
Photo by Karen Bell

" I'm a New Yorker, definitely a city person, and I think this creates an interesting juxtaposition—a contrast between the traditional image of quilting as a part of rural culture and my own urban-shaped existence. "

▲ **Kaleidoscopic XXXIV: The Never-Ending Kaleidoscope (One Block of Twelve)** | 2009
12 x 12 inches (30.5 x 30.5 cm)
Cottons, marbled silk; machine pieced, stretched, framed
Silk by Cosette
Photo by Christina Carty-Francis

" My M.O. is to camouflage seams through fabric manipulation. This establishes an uninterrupted flow of design or color from one fabric patch to the next, creating the illusion that there are no seams at all. "

▲ **Kaleidoscopic XXXIV: The Never-Ending Kaleidoscope (One Block of Twelve)** | 2009
12 x 12 inches (30.5 x 30.5 cm)
Cottons, marbled silk; machine pieced, stretched, framed
Silk by Cosette
Photo by Christina Carty-Francis

▲ Kaleidoscopic XIX: Tulips in the Courtyard Below | 1998

36 x 36 inches (91.4 x 91.4 cm)
Cottons, silk; machine pieced, hand quilted
Photo by Karen Bell

Dirkje van der Horst-Beetsma

AN ARTIST WHO LIKES TO TOY with tradition, Dirkje van der Horst-Beetsma makes quilts that are full of surprises. Her pieces are often covered with thousands of tiny raw-edge appliquéd fabrics. Strips of cloth—which she refers to as flaps—often seem to be coming loose. Van der Horst-Beetsma has made a number of works that feature this evocative peeling-wallpaper effect. All of the flaps are different.

She also makes landscape quilts based on her native Friesland, a province in the Netherlands. Featuring windblown skies and wide, flat fields, their forms aren't divided into standard diptych or triptych formats but are instead composed of unevenly sized vertical sections. These pieces are laced together with unusual materials such as zippers or tire inner tubes.

In contrast, the works that van der Horst-Beetsma has created entirely from stitched lines are whole cloth, and she creates her patterns from repeated rows of tightly formed machine quilting. Instead of hanging still upon the wall, her pieces seem to ripple and undulate. As van der Horst-Beetsma paints with fabric and thread, she consistently overturns expectations, providing viewers with new ways of perceiving the quilt.

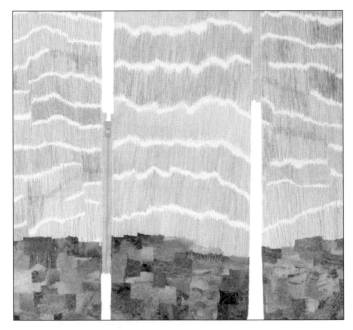

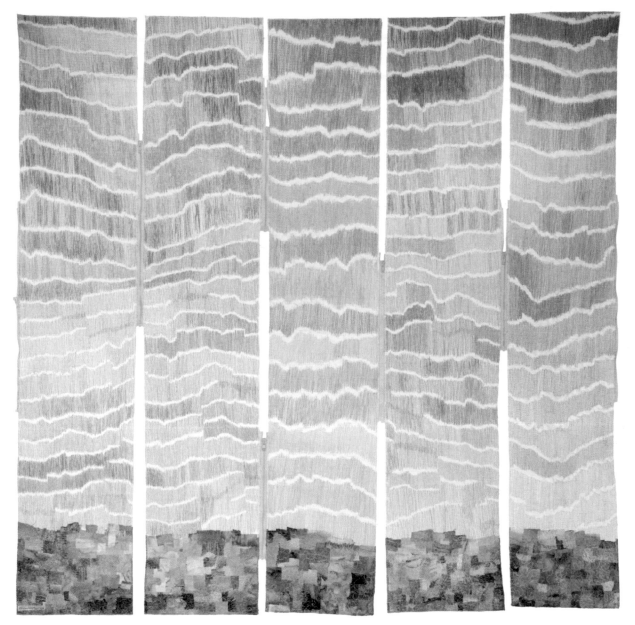

▲ Frisian Sky | 2008

5⅞ x 53¹⁵/₁₆ inches (1.4 x 1.3 m)
Cotton, silk, rayon; hand dyed, appliquéd,
machine sewn

Photos by DPFstudio.com

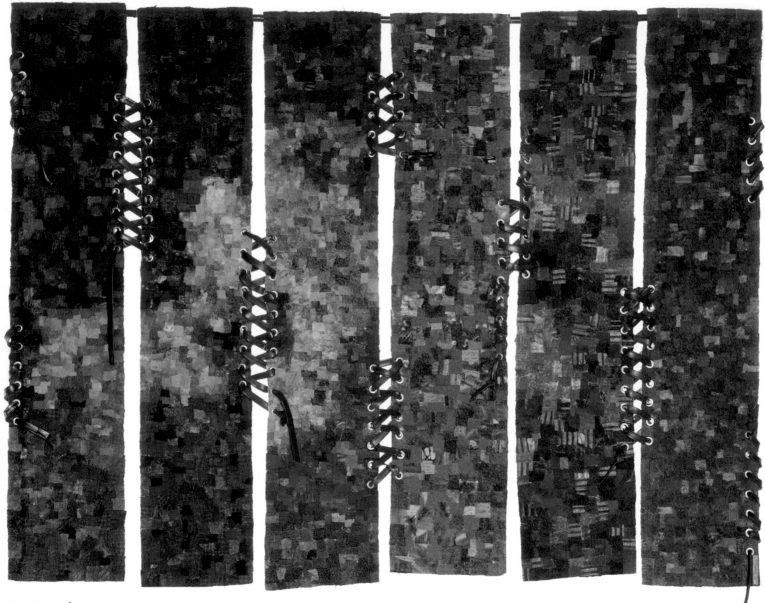

▲ **Tight** | 2007

69⅛ x 98¼ inches (1.7 x 2.5 m)

Cotton, silk, rayon, rubber tubes, metal rings; hand dyed, appliquéd, machine sewn

Photo by DPFstudio.com

" I begin each quilt
with a full-sized
piece of cotton and
an embroidery hoop.
With my machine—
and without using
pins or glue—I stitch
small pieces of fabric
directly onto the
cotton in much the
same way that paint
is directly applied to
a canvas. The hoop
keeps the cotton
stretched and taut. "

◀ **Elseverywhere** | 2002

50¾ x 41⁵⁄₁₆ inches (129 x 105 cm)
Cotton, silk; appliquéd, machine
sewn, embroidered

Photo by DPFstudio.com

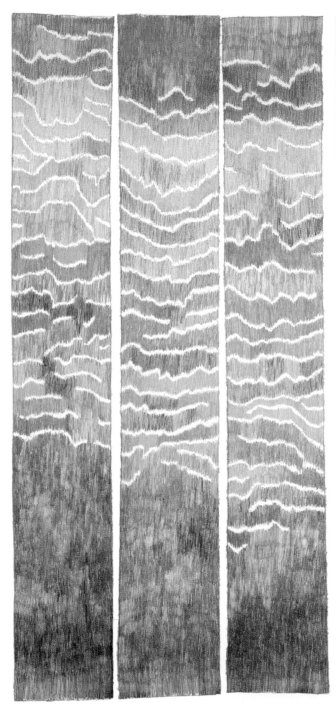

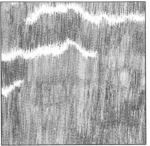

◀ **Aurora** | 2006

58 x 9 inches (1.5 x 0.2 m)
Silk, canvas, cotton thread;
free stitched

Photos by DPFstudio.com

▼ **Galaxy of Memories** | 2003

38 x 56 inches (0.9 x 1.4 m)
Cotton, silk, linen, polyester; photo transfer,
free appliquéd, machine stitched

Photo by DPFstudio.com

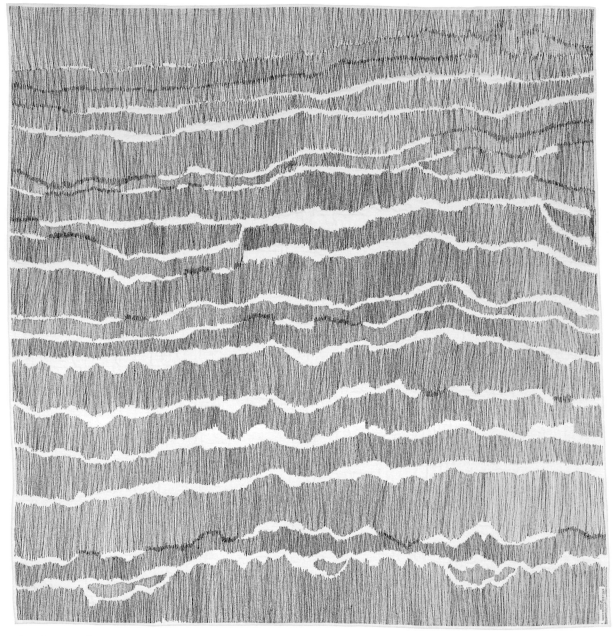

" Inspiration comes from varied sources— words, photographs, patterns on manhole lids, and weathered doors. These artificial forms and textures provide a nice contrast to fabric. "

▲ Allegro | 2001

45¹¹⁄₁₆ x 47¼ inches (116 x 120 cm)

Cotton, whole cloth; machine sewn

Photo by DPFstudio.com

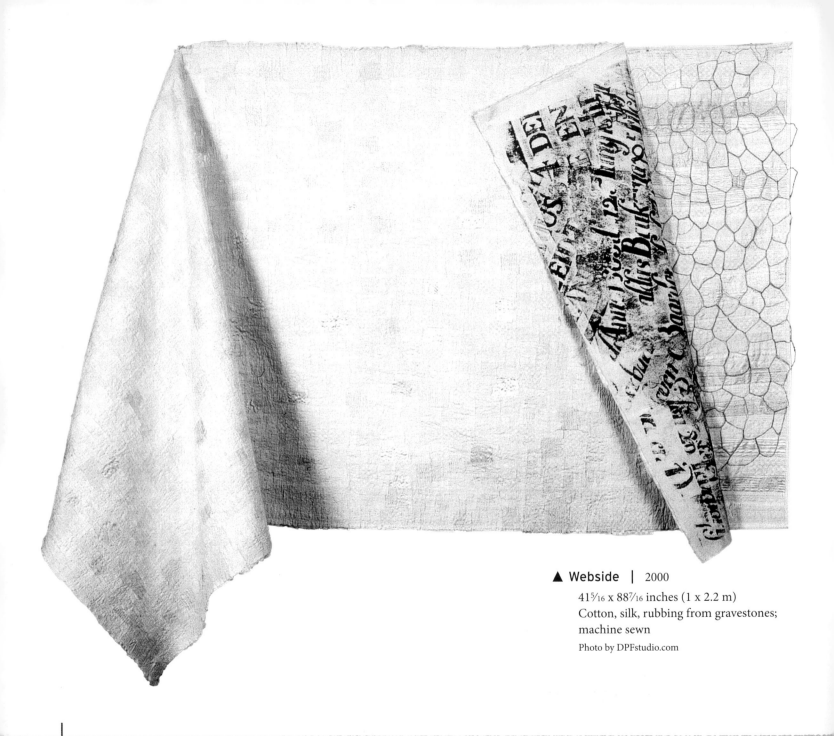

▲ **Webside** | 2000
41⁵⁄₁₆ x 88⁷⁄₁₆ inches (1 x 2.2 m)
Cotton, silk, rubbing from gravestones;
machine sewn

Photo by DPFstudio.com

" My quilts are abstract and often feature raw-edged appliqué. These raw pieces usually don't have a binding, and when I exhibit them, people often think I didn't have enough time to finish the work. The truth is I just don't like binding. "

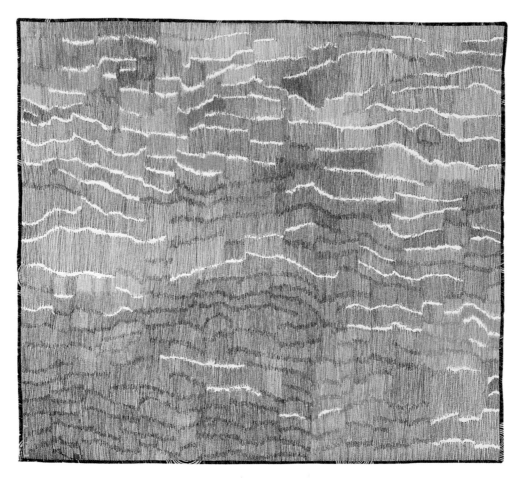

▲ Vivace | 2006

37 x 41 inches (95 x 105 cm)
Silk, cotton thread, canvas; free stitched
Photo by DPFstudio.com

▲ Cobblestones | 1999

59¾ x 51³⁄₁₆ inches (1.5 x 1.3 m)

Cotton, silk, linen, rayon; hand dyed, appliquéd, machine sewn

Photo by DPFstudio.com

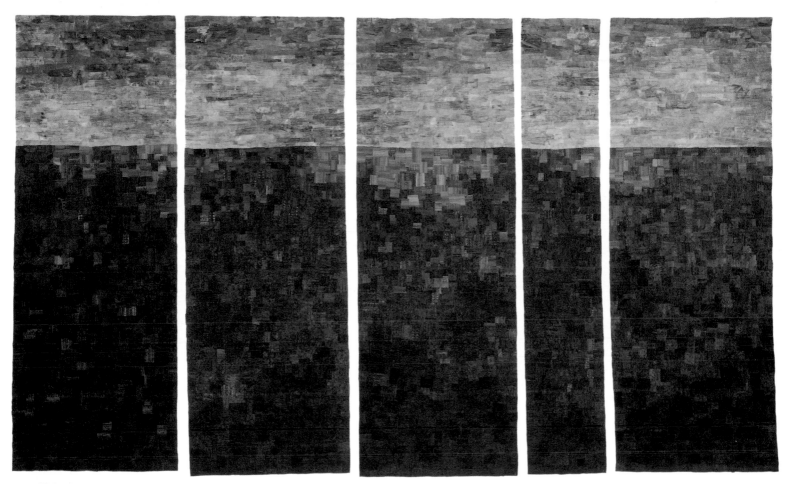

▲ **Frisian Landscape** | 2009

67⁹/₁₆ x 107¹¹/₁₆ inches (1.7 x 2.7 m)
Cotton, silk, linen; hand dyed,
appliquéd, machine sewn, painted

Photos by DPFstudio.com

Rosalie Dace

CONTRASTS DELIGHT Rosalie Dace. She creates remarkable quilts that are filled with fascinating juxtapositions. Featuring unexpected pairings of textures, colors, and design elements, her work never fails to engage the viewer.

Dace plays up the contrasts between fabrics, teaming the smooth with the rough, the matte with the shiny. She combines tiny, tightly pieced shapes with sweeping quilted arcs. Although they feature mixtures of brocade, cotton, linen, silk, and velvet, each of Dace's quilts is unified by the concept she's trying to express.

Dace finds inspiration all around her—in personal events, world news, and the changing of the seasons. Her quilts are primarily pieced, with highlights such as small gold discs or silver pieced squares that have rich glowing tones and lead the viewer's eye around the surface of the work. Dace's machine quilting creates networks of lines that give each piece wonderful energy. Living at the southern tip of Africa, Dace wishes to capture a sense of her country as a melting pot, redolent with the smell of sought-after spices, the magic of the East, and the mystery of Africa.

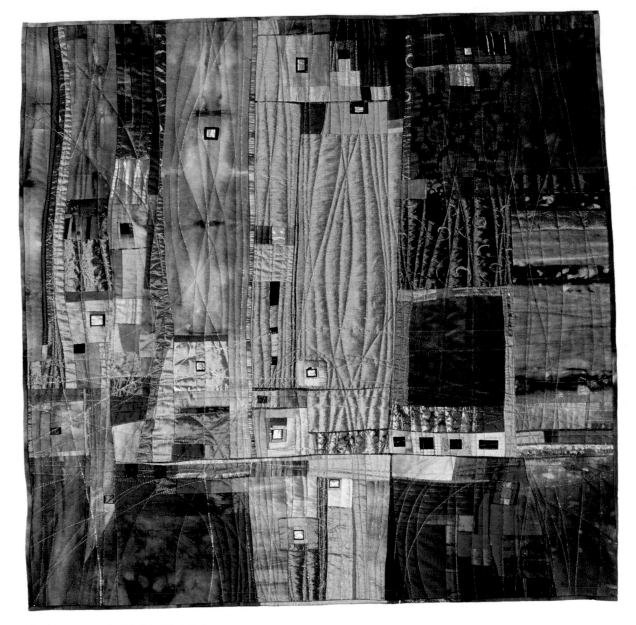

▲ **Journeys 4: Night Flight** | 2007

37¹³⁄₁₆ x 30¹¹⁄₁₆ inches (96 x 78 cm)
Cotton, silk, velvet, taffeta; machine
pieced, hand appliquéd, machine quilted
Photos by George Tadden

47¼ x 34¼ inches (120 x 87 cm)
Cotton, velvet, silk, linen, brocade,
sheers; machine pieced, hand pieced,
hand appliquéd, machine quilted
Photo by George Tadden

" The only class I was
ever thrown out of in
high school was sewing!
I like to tell students
this to remind them
that everyone must
start somewhere. "

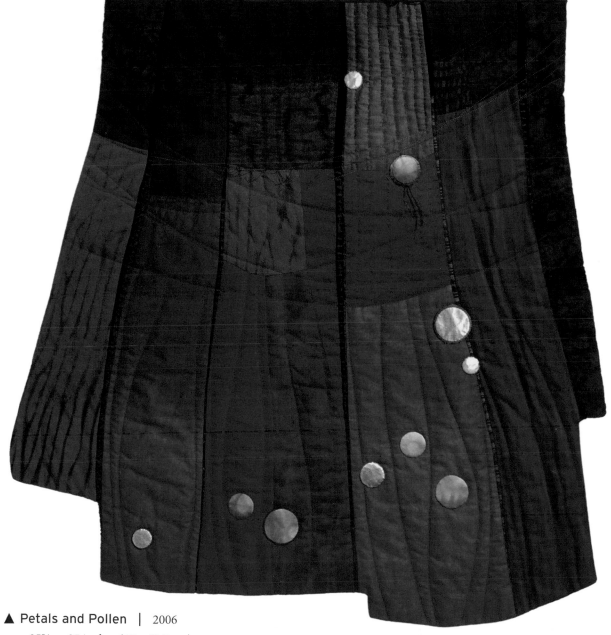

▲ Petals and Pollen | 2006

25⁹/₁₆ x 25 inches (65 x 63.5 cm)
Cotton, silk, brocade, tulle netting; machine pieced,
hand appliquéd, machine quilted, hand quilted
Photo by George Tadden

" Durban, South Africa, where I live, has a very large Indian population that brings a rich depth and color to the local culture through its saris, fabrics, and spices. These things definitely inform my work. "

Moon Woman | 2001 ▶
37³⁄₈ x 18¹⁄₂ inches (95 x 47 cm)
Cotton, brocade, sheers, beads, sequins, metallic thread; machine appliquéd, machine quilted, hand embellished
Photos by George Tadden

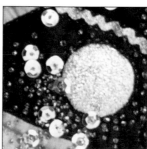

▲ **Let the Sun Shine** | 2001

26 x 38½ inches (66 x 89 cm)
Cotton, silk brocade, braid, sequins, piping;
hand appliquéd, quilted, embellished, embroidered,
machine pieced

Photos by George Tadden

◀ **Earthday** | 2009

56⁵⁄₁₆ x 38¹⁵⁄₁₆ inches (1.4 x 0.9 m)
Cotton, silk, velvet, sheers,
metallic threads; machine pieced,
hand appliquéd, machine quilted,
hand quilted

Photos by George Tadden

▲ **Durban Dreams** | 2005

26¾ x 27¹⁵⁄₁₆ inches (68 x 71 cm)
Cotton, silk, synthetics, beads, buttons;
machine pieced, machine quilted,
hand embellished

Photo by George Tadden

" Art quilting spans the indefinable, magical area between painting and sculpture. "

◀ **Journeys 3: Spice Route** | 2006

35⁷⁄₁₆ x 26¾ inches (90 x 68 cm)
Cotton, silk, velvet, brocade, metallic
thread; machine pieced, machine
appliquéd, machine quilted

Photos by George Tadden

Watching and Waiting | 2005 ▶

55⅛ x 47⅝ inches (1.4 x 1.2 m)
Cotton, silk, organza, metallic thread;
machine pieced, machine appliquéd,
machine quilted

Photo by George Tadden

▲ Awake My Soul | 2001

49³/₁₆ x 45¼ inches (125 x 115 cm)

Cotton, silk, sheers; machine pieced, machine appliquéd, machine quilted

Photo by George Tadden

Leslie Gabriëlse

ALTHOUGH THEY'RE SURROUNDED by bright colors and cheerful patterns, the men and women featured in Leslie Gabriëlse's quilts often seem pensive and distracted. Gabriëlse excels at capturing ambiguous emotional moments, and his work often straddles the border between reality and illusion. His "fabric paintings" are created through raw-edge appliqué. Colors are enhanced or blended by the judicious use of acrylic paint. Backgrounds are created from a simple frame of fabric swatches. Each fabric edge is meticulously sewn down with large, decorative hand-stitches using #5 Perle cotton thread.

Gabriëlse, who lives in the Netherlands, had his first success with fabric portraits of members of Rotterdam's artistic community. Working from small preliminary sketches in watercolor or charcoal, he created finished quilts that were often life-size or larger. He has since worked in other genres, producing abstract textile pieces filled with light and bright color.

At first glance, his striking portraits seem realistic, but closer observation reveals surprises—a partially blue face or plaid hair. It's through these skillful manipulations of abstraction and realism that Gabriëlse transforms the world—and our way of seeing it.

On Holiday | 1979 ▶

94½ x 59¹/₁₆ inches (2.4 x 1.5 m)
Fabric, hand sewn

Photos by artist

▲ Artists II | 1982

77¹⁵⁄₁₆ x 109⁷⁄₁₆ inches (1.9 x 2.7 m)
Fabric, charcoal, acrylic paint; hand sewn

Photo by artist

" I'm very drawn to commercial fabrics. I'm fascinated by
the variety of motifs and textures they have to offer. "

Magician II | 1982 ▶

79 x 161 inches (2 x 4.1 m)
Fabric; hand sewn

Photos by artist

◀ **Dance Break** | 1983

87⁷⁄₁₆ x 116¹⁄₈ inches (2.2 x 2.9 m)
Fabric, acrylic paint; hand sewn

Photos by artist

▲ Together in a Boat | 1983
68¹⁵⁄₁₆ x 94½ inches (1.7 x 2.4 m)
Fabric, acrylic paint; hand sewn
Photo by artist

" I create preparatory drawings and use acrylic paint to suggest the directions of color and light. Sometimes I rely on these sketches to guide me in the final application process, but I always leave room for improvisation. "

◀ Mariette Fetter | 1995
70 x 32 inches (1.7 x 0.8 m)
Fabric, acrylic paint;
hand sewn
Photos by artist

" I use a variety of hand stitches to enhance my surfaces and add tactility. My subjects are quite varied, ranging from figures and still lifes to non-representational compositions. "

You and Me III | 2006 ▶
60 x 36 inches (1.5 x 0.9 m)
Fabric, acrylic paint;
hand sewn
Photo by artist

LESLIE GABRIËLSE

▲ **Swimming** | 1999

59 1/16 x 78 3/4 inches (1.5 x 2 m)

Fabric, acrylic paint; hand sewn

Photo by artist

▲ Caroline and Hans Giebing | 2005

39³⁄₈ x 33¹⁄₂ inches (100 x 85 cm)
Fabric, acrylic paint; hand sewn
Photos by artist

▲ **Woman with Two Gents** | 2001
59 1/16 x 76 13/16 inches (1.5 x 1.9 m)
Fabric, acrylic paint; hand sewn
Photo by artist

Nelda Warkentin

WINDS BLOW, BRANCHES SWAY, birds flutter, and leaves turn: Nature's beauty is crystallized into abstractions of color, line, and light in the quilts of Nelda Warkentin. Much of Warkentin's imagery is drawn from her home state of Alaska, but she's also stimulated by travel and new locales. Vacations in Mexico inspired visions of palm trees and tropical birds, while an artist's residency in Connecticut provided the interplay of verticals found in fences and tree trunks. The locations may vary, but Warkentin finds nature's repetition of pattern and form to be a constant source of inspiration.

To capture the beauty she sees around her, Warkentin begins with a base of heavy artist's canvas, which she transforms with layer upon layer of transparent painted silk. She works in repeating units that give each quilt a sense of rhythm. The units are similar yet different. Gently curving lines often contrast with the strict geometrical form of the square. Machine quilting swirls across each quilt, sometimes reinforced with colored pencil.

The interplay of color and light engages the viewer. From the layers of painted silk, Warkentin creates luminous blues, greens, purples, and reds that magically coalesce. Amidst the bands of color, light sparkles and glows—reflections of nature's glory.

▲ Sea Ice | 2008
36 x 36 inches (91.4 x 91.4 cm)
Silk, cotton, canvas, cotton batting; painted, machine sewn, machine quilted
Photos by John Tuckey

▲ Tropical Dream | 2002

60 x 48 inches (152.4 x 121.9 cm)
Silk, linen, cotton, canvas, cotton batting; painted,
machine sewn, machine quilted

Photo by John Tuckey

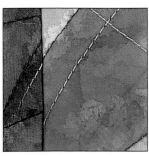

▲ **Zephyr** | 2007

20 x 30 inches (50.8 x 76.2 cm)
Silk, linen, cotton, cotton canvas,
cotton batting; painted, machine
sewn, machine quilted

Photos by John Tuckey

" I prefer quilting to other mediums, such
as painting or photography, because I like
constructing images. Putting pieces together to
make a whole intrigues and challenges me. "

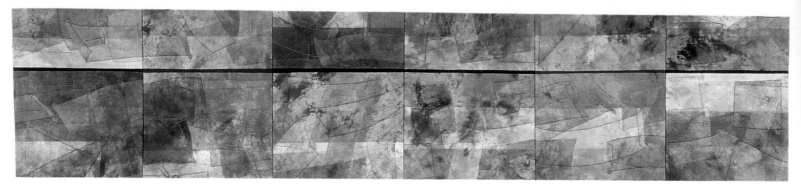

▲ Blue Line | 2004

12 x 54 inches (30.5 x 137.2 cm)
Silk, linen, cotton, canvas, cotton batting;
painted, machine sewn, machine quilted

Photo by John Tuckey

" My work is about color, rhythm, pattern, and symmetry.
The design elements found in nature—the curved line of a
palm frond, the straight line of the horizon—all inspire me. **"**

Glacier Rendezvous II | 2007 ▶

36 x 60 inches (91.4 x 152.4 cm)
Silk, cotton, canvas, linen, acrylic
paint; machine constructed
and quilted

Photo by John Tuckey

▲ Pond's Edge | 2008

36 x 36 inches (91.4 x 91.4 cm)
Silk, cotton, canvas, cotton batting; painted,
machine sewn, machine quilted

Photo by John Tuckey

◀ **Early Spring, East Hill** | 2006
56 x 40 inches (142.2 x 101.6 cm)
Silk, linen, cotton, canvas,
cotton batting; painted,
machine sewn, machine quilted
Photo by John Tuckey

▲ Glacier Rendezvous | 2006

41 x 30 inches (104.1 x 76.2 cm)
Silk, cotton, canvas, cotton batting;
painted, machine sewn, machine quilted

Photo by John Tuckey

Blue Tulips | 2009 ▶

33 x 11 inches (83.8 x 27.9 cm)
Silk, cotton, canvas, acrylic paint;
machine constructed and quilted

Photo by John Tuckey

▲ **Palms Swaying, Whales Breaching** | 2005

50 x 40 inches (127 x 101.6 cm)
Silk, cotton, linen, canvas; painted,
machine constructed, machine quilted

Photo by John Tuckey

▲ **Bird of Paradise** | 2008

46 x 69 inches (116.8 x 175.3 cm)
Silk, cotton, canvas, cotton batting;
painted, machine sewn, machine quilted
Photo by John Tuckey

" I work in layers in order to achieve a painterly
quality and create images with depth. I view my
quilts as layered paintings. "

Gayle Fraas
& Duncan Slade

EVERYONE HAS MEMORIES of a favorite place. Tapping into the unique connection we all feel for special locales is what Gayle Fraas and Duncan Slade do in their remarkable work. Combining realistic landscape portraiture with complex framing elements, they create quilts that convey the essence of place. These multifaceted quilts also provide viewers with different ways of looking at a single scene—both literally and symbolically.

Fraas and Slade paint their landscapes with thickened fiber-reactive dyes, repainting each area as many as four times in order to achieve depth and luminosity.

They create border patterns separately on paper with gouache, pastel, and charcoal and then transfer the patterns to fabric using digital printing.

Fraas and Slade quilt by machine and by hand. Islands and water views near their home in Maine provide rich inspiration for their work. Nautical signal flags prompted a recent series of quilts—poignant pieces that explore themes of travel and experience. As with much of Fraas and Slade's work, these quilts reference the universal yearning to find a way back home.

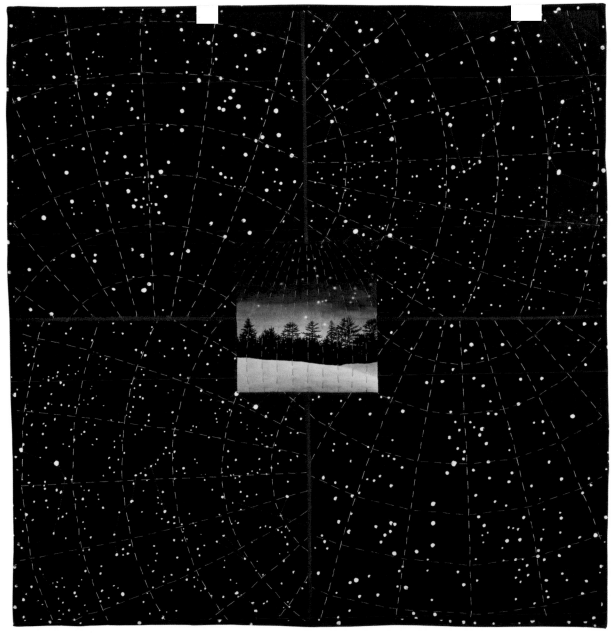

▲ **Last Day of the Year** | 2009

24 x 24 inches (61 x 61 cm)
Cotton; dye painted, machine stitched, hand stitched
Photos by Dennis Griggs

▲ North Woods Suite: Woods | 2002

28 x 125 inches (0.7 x 3.1 m)
Cotton, fiber-reactive dyes, metal foil;
painted, printed, machine sewn,
hand sewn

Photos by Dennis Griggs

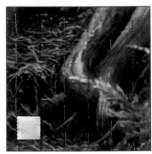

" One of the first things we learned from our
mothers was the great versatility of a sewing
machine. Textiles in many ways are our
native tongue. **"**

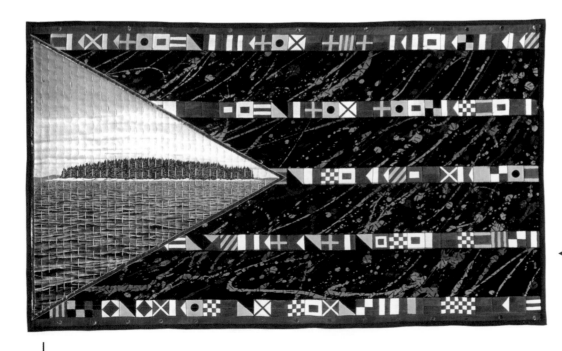

◄ Flag: Local Waters | 2004

18 x 30 inches (45.7 x 76.2 cm)
Cotton, metal foil; dye painted,
machine stitched, hand stitched

Photo by Dennis Griggs

▲ **North Woods Suite: Waterfall** | 2002

77 x 77 inches (1.9 x 1.9 m)
Cotton, metal foil; dye painted, machine stitched,
hand stitched
Photo by Dennis Griggs

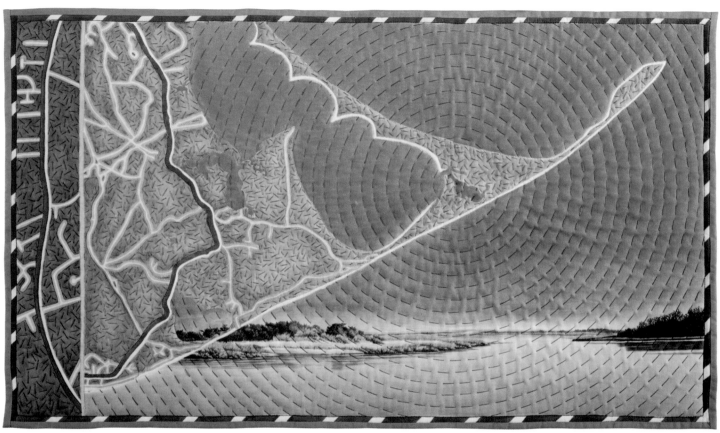

▲ Flag: Coskata | 2008

18 x 30 inches (45.7 x 76.2 cm)
Cotton, fiber-reactive dyes; painted,
machine sewn, hand sewn

Photos by Dennis Griggs

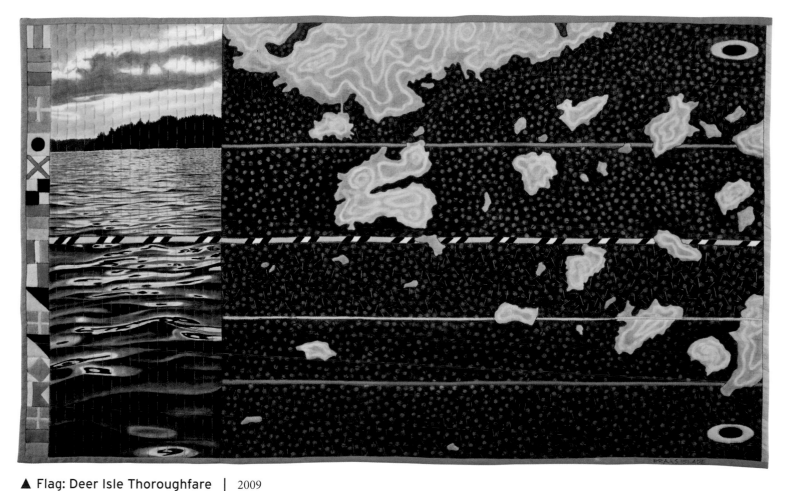

▲ Flag: Deer Isle Thoroughfare | 2009

18 x 30 inches (45.7 x 76.2 cm)
Cotton, fiber-reactive dyes; resist, painted,
machine sewn, hand sewn

Photo by Dennis Griggs

" Aesthetically, the two of us travel the same road. The exits one of us may choose to take—by introducing new materials, or trying out a new process—always seem to lead back to that shared path. "

▲ **Between Two Rivers: The Edgecomb Suite—Colby Preserve** | 2003

40 x 40 inches (101.6 x 101.6 cm)

Cotton, fiber-reactive dyes; painted, printed, machine sewn, hand sewn

Photo by Dennis Griggs

▲ **Between Two Rivers: The Edgecomb Suite–Schmid Preserve** | 2003

40 x 40 inches (101.6 x 101.6 cm)
Cotton, fiber-reactive dyes; painted, printed, machine sewn, hand sewn
Photo by Dennis Griggs

▲ Two | 2009
20 x 40 inches (50.8 x 101.6 cm)
Cotton, fiber-reactive dyes; painted,
machine sewn, hand sewn
Photo by Dennis Griggs

" We have an interest in duration—in the time
it takes a viewer to visually move through a
composition. Like musicians, we attempt to hold
our audience's attention through changes in tone,
tempo, and volume. "

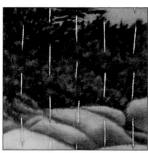

▲ **Flag: Merchant's Row** | 2008

18 x 30 inches (45.7 x 76.2 cm)
Cotton, fiber-reactive dyes; painted,
machine sewn, hand sewn

Photos by Dennis Griggs

Dianne Firth

THE RIPPLING, CONCENTRIC LINES featured in Dianne Firth's quilts have a calming, nearly hypnotic effect upon the viewer—a quality that seems at odds with the harsh natural landscape of Australia, which provides the main inspiration for her work. But Firth, who has served as head of the landscape architecture department at the University of Canberra, views her environment through an analytical framework. In her art she pares landscapes, waterways, and plants down to their elemental qualities. She sketches out her scenes instead of working from photographs, because the act of drawing helps her understand the essence of what she's observing.

Firth's creative techniques depend upon the qualities she's trying to convey. She uses machine piecing when she wants to be precise but loves the tactile qualities created by unraveled raw edges. She uses a wide range of materials, including fabrics, leaves, plastics—even paper clips. One of her recurring themes is the ephemeral nature of water and the ways in which it affects the environment.

Through unforgettable quilts that capture the essential qualities of the landscape—its subtle differences in tone and texture—Firth re-imagines the world in new and wonderful ways.

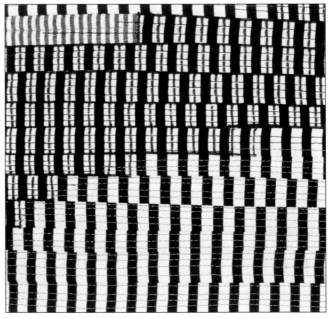

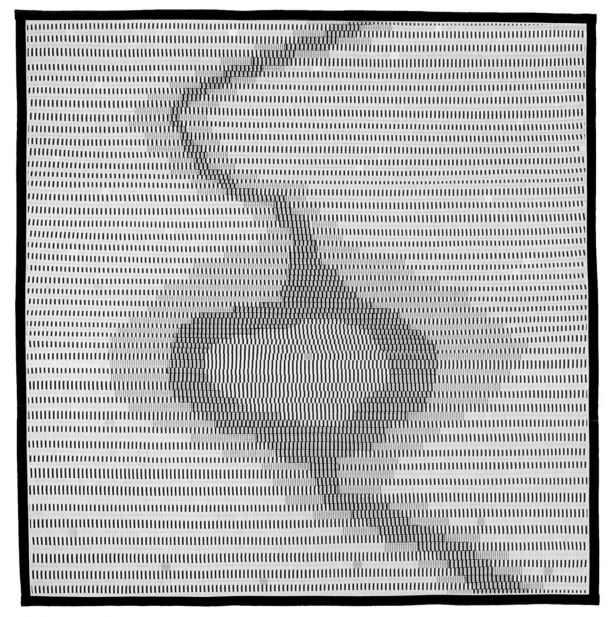

▲ The Soak | 2005

58¹⁵⁄₁₆ x 58¹⁵⁄₁₆ inches (1.5 x 1.5 m)
Cotton; strip pieced, machine sewn,
machine quilted, painted
Photos by David Paterson

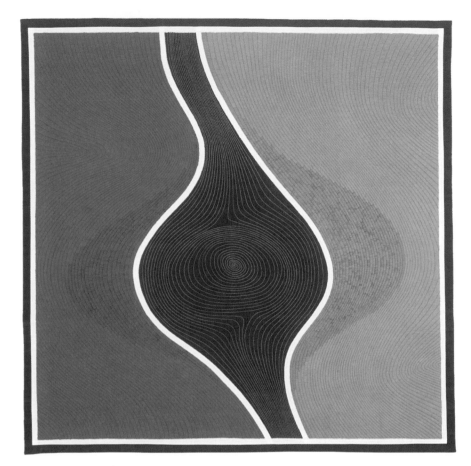

▲ **The Flood** | 2005

58¹⁵⁄₁₆ x 58¹⁵⁄₁₆ inches (1.5 x 1.5 m)
Cotton; machine pieced, machine quilted, painted

Photo by David Paterson

" Through my work, I try to develop new ways of seeing that will

encourage the viewer to look at the landscape in a different way. "

◀ **Cell Structure #7** | 2007

52¾ x 29⅛ inches (1.3 x 0.7 m)
Wool felt; reverse appliquéd,
machine quilted
Photo by Andrew Sikorski

◀ **Red River Flowing** | 2005

$54\frac{5}{16}$ x $18\frac{1}{2}$ inches (1.3 x 0.4 m)
Cotton; torn-strip appliquéd, machine
quilted, screen printed, painted

Photo by Andrew Sikorski

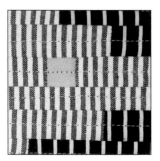

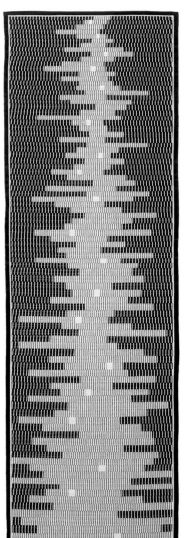

Reflections #2 | 2006 ▶

$52\frac{3}{4}$ x $16\frac{15}{16}$ inches (1.3 x 0.4 m)
Cotton; machine pieced,
machine quilted

Photos by artist

" I try to project a minimal structure in my work, but I also incorporate specific detail elements and embellishments—colored thread or painted highlights—to enhance a close viewing of each piece. "

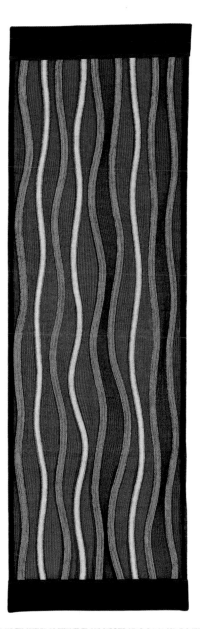

▲ **Water Forms** | 2009

Left: 42⅛ x 39¾ inches (107 x 101 cm)
Right: 56¹¹⁄₁₆ x 17⁵⁄₁₆ inches (1.4 x 0.4 m)

Polyester net, cotton, viscose felt;
torn-strip appliquéd, machine quilted, painted

Photos by David Paterson

▲ Field | 2008

56⅝16 x 54¹¹⁄₁₆ inches (1.4 x 1.3 m)

Cotton; torn-strip appliquéd, machine quilted, painted

Photo by Andrew Sikorski

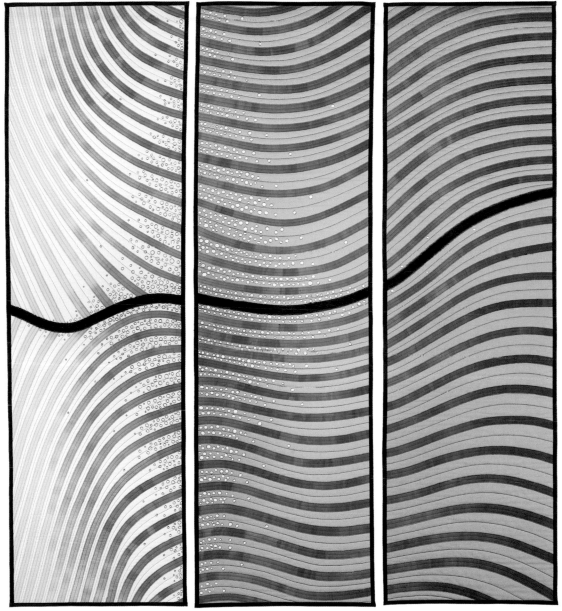

> " I've worked with other media, but the quilt is now my preference. It gives me the ability to express ideas in new ways beyond the dominant paradigm of paint on canvas. "

▲ Coast | 2007

55⅛ x 50⅜ inches (1.4 x 1.2 m)
Cotton; torn-strip appliquéd, machine quilted, hand dyed, painted
Photo by David Paterson

DIANNE FIRTH

◄ **Upland** | 2007

55⅛ x 42⅞ inches (1.4 x 1 m)
Cotton; torn-strip appliquéd,
machine quilted, hand dyed,
painted

Photo by David Paterson

DIANNE FIRTH

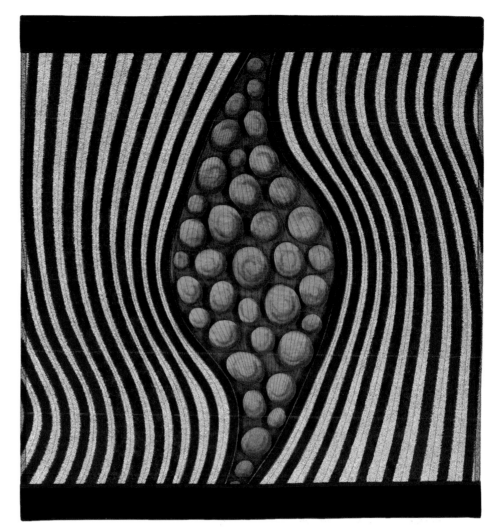

◀ **Water Collection** | 2009

Left: 56¹¹⁄₁₆ x 17⁵⁄₁₆ inches (1.4 x 0.4 m)
Right: 42⅛ x 39¾ inches (107 x 101 cm)

Cotton, viscose felt, polyester net; reverse appliquéd,
torn-strip appliquéd, machine quilted, painted

Photos by David Paterson

Reiko Naganuma

AN ARTIST WHO CLEARLY DELIGHTS in her medium, Reiko Naganuma crafts quilts that are intricate dances of strong geometric shapes and bold color. Stylized trees, flowers, and people are featured in many of her pieces, while other works focus on pure geometric forms. Naganuma often hand weaves her own fabrics, and she achieves a wide variety of textures in her quilts through the use of different materials, including denim, silk, and kimono fabric. The harmonious integration of different fiber types and weights gives her surfaces a unique richness.

Naganuma, who lives in Japan, employs innovative techniques to construct her quilts. She often pieces fabrics together so that they make a block, which she then slices into, pulling the block open along its cut edges and sewing it down into a new configuration. By opening up pieced elements in this way, Naganuma reveals her background colors and creates fascinating secondary patterns. With machine quilting and embroidery stitches, she meticulously highlights each part of her design.

Naganuma's vibrant quilts always reward close inspection. They are full of charming stitched surprises.

▲ **Autumn Sky** | 2008

80³/₁₆ x 68³/₄ inches (2 x 1.7 m)
Cotton, linen, nylon, organza; machine
pieced, quilted, appliquéd, embroidered

Photos by Masaru Nomura

▲ **Dance! Dance! II** | 2001

84⅞ x 71⅛ inches (2.1 x 1.8 m)
Cotton; machine pieced, quilted,
appliquéd, embroidered

Photos by Masaru Nomura

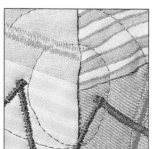

▲ **New Morning** | 1999

61⅝₁₆ x 74¹¹⁄₁₆ inches (1.5 x 1.9 m)
Cotton; machine pieced, quilted,
appliquéd, embroidered

Photos by Masaru Nomura

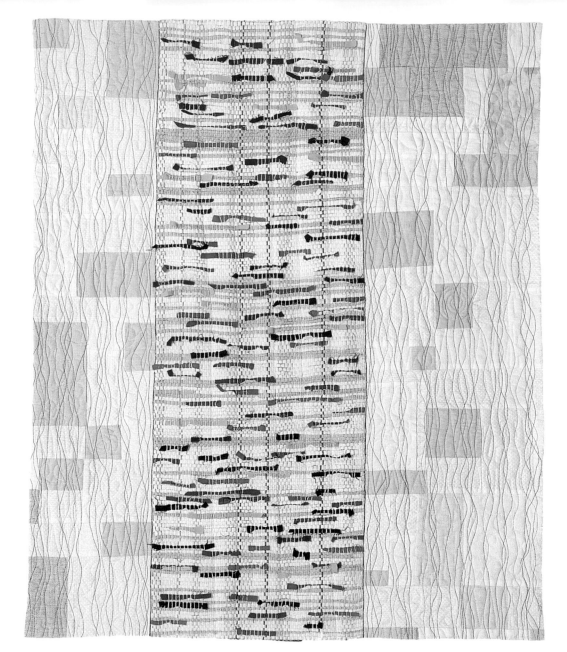

▲ In a Dream | 2009

38⁹/₁₆ x 31⁷/₈ inches (98 x 81 cm)

Cotton, wool; machine pieced, machine quilted

Photo by Masaru Nomura

" To make works
like *Slit* and
Autumn Sky, I
start by making
a flat quilt and
add quilting on
top. This gives
the piece a three-
dimensional
quality and
emphasizes
the shapes I've
designed. "

▲ **Slit** | 2005
79 x 79 inches (2 x 2 m)
Cotton, linen, denim; machine pieced, quilted
Photo by Masaru Nomura

▲ Orange Moon | 2003

75¹³⁄₁₆ x 75¹³⁄₁₆ inches (1.9 x 1.9 m)

Cotton, denim; hand dyed, machine pieced, machine quilted, machine embroidered, hand embroidered

Photo by Masaru Nomura

" When I start making a quilt, I draw a simple design of the theme, then do some brainstorming about the fabrics I might use. In the later stages of the work—adding the quilting lines and embroidery—I add complexity and create extra layers of texture. "

▲ Door | 2003

80⁹⁄₁₆ x 66¹³⁄₁₆ inches (2 x 1.7 m)
Cotton, linen, polyester; machine pieced, quilted, appliquéd, embroidered, hand painted, hand embroidered
Photos by Masaru Nomura

▲ **The Summer Days** | 2003

51³⁄₁₆ x 51³⁄₁₆ inches (1.3 x 1.3 m)
Cotton, linen, polyester; machine
pieced, quilted, appliquéd

Photo by Masaru Nomura

" In 2006 I learned how to hand weave and began using my own hand-woven fabrics in my quilts. I try to incorporate unusual fibers like kiwi vines and slubbed yarns into my textiles. "

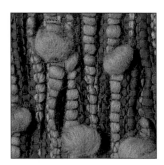

The Summer Sun | 2006 ▶

83¹¹⁄₁₆ x 67⁵⁄₈ inches (2.1 x 1.7 m)
Cotton, linen, polyester, denim,
silk; machine pieced, quilted,
embroidered

Photos by Masaru Nomura

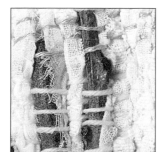

A Scorching Sun | 2007 ▶

85¼ x 65¼ inches (217 x 166 cm)
Cotton, linen, nylon, organza;
machine pieced, quilted,
appliquéd, embroidered

Photos by Masaru Nomura

Shulamit Liss

A BROODING PALETTE that includes ocher, black, gray, and brown predominates in the atmospheric work of Shulamit Liss. Her densely textured quilts are dark, but hints of vibrant color often burst through. To achieve the complex, deep patterning that her quilts feature, Liss uses arashi shibori, discharge, stamping, and other printing techniques. Her work celebrates both the richness and the loss that define all of our lives.

Liss pieces and quilts her work by machine, often printing over her quilting lines to add additional layers of patterning. She uses strips of pleated fabric to create areas of light and shadow. Sometimes the pleats symbolize personal or social barriers and seem like bars. In other pieces, the pleats represent softly rolling hills captured in the fading light of the evening sun.

Liss, who lives in Israel, is inspired by the countryside. Primarily abstract in her designs, she often experiments with the addition of realistic stamped motifs including cows, doves, and skulls. Influenced by both rural and urban landscapes, Liss is fascinated by the play of light across a scene—and with the contradictions that make up daily life.

▲ Falling Leaves | 2007

    $66^{13}/_{16}$ x $58^{15}/_{16}$ inches (1.7 x 1.5 m)
    Cotton; hand dyed, bleached, painted,
    printed, appliquéd, machine sewn
    Photos by Avraham Hay

" The quilt medium
fits my personality.
It combines quick
thinking and creativity
with patience and
an appreciation for
handicraft. "

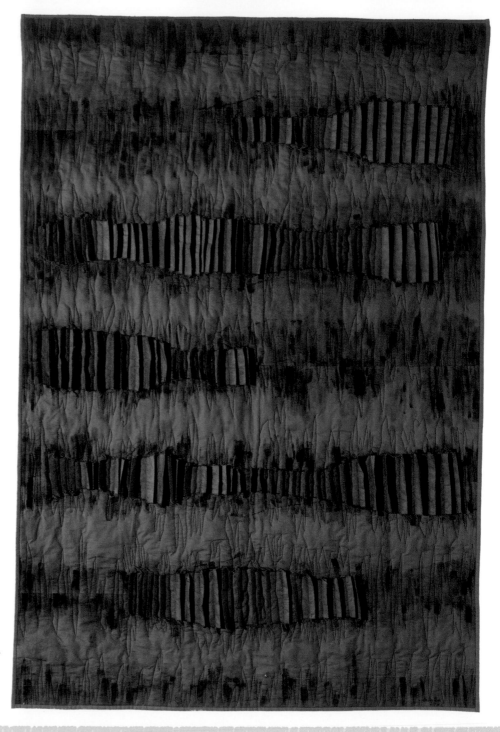

SHULAMIT LISS

Landscape in Gray | 2001 ▶
66¹³⁄₁₆ x 45¼ inches (1.7 x 1.1 m)
Cotton; painted, folded
Photo by Avraham Hay

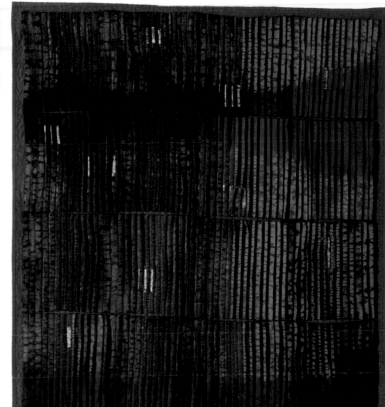

▲ **Memorial Pictures** | 1998

$46^{13}/_{16}$ x $41^{3}/_{4}$ inches (119 x 106 cm)
Cotton; hand dyed, reverse appliquéd,
printed, machine sewn
Photos by Avraham Hay

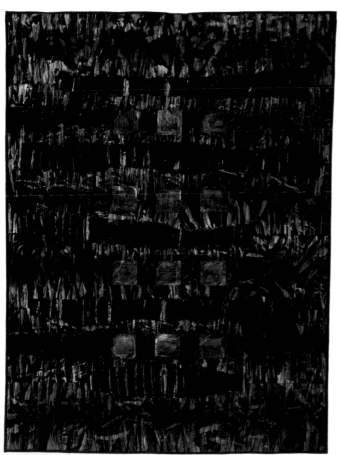

◄ **Earth** | 2001

$69^{9}/_{16}$ x $50^{7}/_{8}$ inches (1.7 x 1.3 m)
Cotton; hand dyed, bleached,
painted, printed
Photo by Avraham Hay

▲ **Red Center** | 2004

59¾ x 75½ inches (1.5 x 1.9 m)
Cotton; hand dyed, bleached, painted, appliquéd, embroidered, machine sewn

Photo by Avraham Hay

" I try to embed into
my work the two
philosophical layers we
all live in—the present
realistic layer and the
past hidden layer. "

▲ Almost Summer | 2007
55⅞ x 48¹³⁄₁₆ inches (1.4 x 1.2 m)
Cotton; hand dyed, bleached, painted, appliquéd, machine sewn
Photo by Avraham Hay

▲ **Eight Cows** | 2000

28⁵⁄₁₆ x 66¹³⁄₁₆ inches (0.7 x 1.7 m)
Cotton; hand dyed, bleached, painted, printed,
machine sewn

Photo by Avraham Hay

" I often paint, dye, and print my fabrics under a big tree
in my yard, using leaves, grass, stones, and branches
for the coloring process. The results are completely
different from what I get when I work in my studio. **"**

▲ Torn Bars II | 1999

55½ x 44⅛6 inches (1.4 x 1.1 m)
Cotton; hand dyed, bleached, printed,
embroidered, folded, machine sewn

Photos by Avraham Hay

▲ **Singing in Caesarea** | 2005

47⅝ x 55⅞ inches (1.2 x 1.4 m)
Cotton; hand dyed, bleached, painted,
printed, appliquéd, machine sewn

Photo by Avraham Hay

Dreaming Peace | 2006 ▶

35⁷⁄₁₆ x 23⁵⁄₈ inches (90 x 60 cm)
Cotton; printed, appliquéd,
machine sewn

Photos by Avrahama Hay

SHULAMIT **LISS**

Alice Beasley

DURING HER LONG CAREER AS A LAWYER in San Francisco, Alice Beasley often had to take cartons of documents and distill the information they contained into persuasive contracts or arguments. In her artwork she goes through a similar process, crystallizing key moments so that viewers are captivated by a person's emotional state or by the exquisite beauty of a still life.

Beasley prefers fabrics with prints because they blend together visually. She doesn't use paint or dye. She free-hand cuts her material without the use of a pattern or visual aid. To create realistic-looking images, she uses raw-edge appliqué with minimal machine quilting.

Beasley's handling of color is masterful, and her shadows—often composed from textiles that are completely different from her main fabric—are intriguing. In each of Beasley's portraits and still lifes, the elements seem to have been perfectly composed in order to capture the subject's essential nature.

▲ **Home Street Home** | 1994

49 x 57 inches (1.2 x 1.4 m)

Cotton; machine appliquéd, machine sewn

Photos by Jim Jacobs

Bail Me | 2009 ▶

37 x 28 inches (94 x 71.1 cm)
Cotton; thread work, appliquéd,
machine sewn

Photos by Don Tuttle

" I would call my style objective realism. I love the challenge of making recognizable people and objects and being able to draw meaning from their depiction. "

◀ Miles Ahead | 2006

47½ x 24 inches (120.7 x 61 cm)
Cotton, silk; appliquéd, machine sewn

Photos by Don Tuttle

◀ El Cubano | 2005

41 x 30 inches (104.1 x 76.2 cm)
Cotton; appliquéd, machine sewn
Photo by Don Tuttle

Bette's Diner | 1998 ▶

44½ x 59 inches (1.1 x 1.5 m)
Cotton, iridescent fabrics;
machine appliquéd,
machine sewn
Photos by Jim Jacobs

" In many of my pieces, parts of figures—a toe,
an elbow, a section of some object—poke out
of the frame. It's as if they're trying to insert
themselves into our world or pull us into theirs. "

◀ **Farmer's Market** | 2007

36 x 30 inches (91.4 x 76.2 cm)
Cotton on collar interfacing;
appliquéd, machine sewn
Photo by Don Tuttle

▲ **Mimi's Pomegranates** | 2008

23 x 23 inches (58.4 x 58.4 cm)
Cotton, silk; machine appliquéd, machine sewn

Photo by Don Tuttle

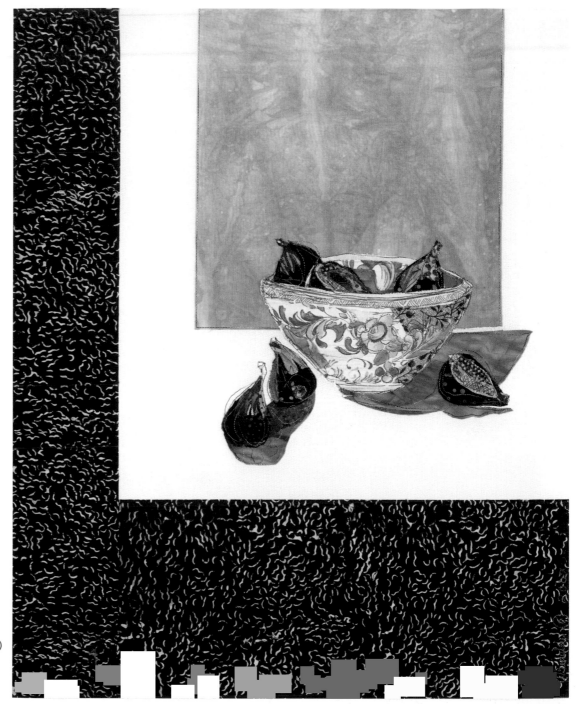

Mission Figs | 2007 ▶

21 x 17 inches (53.3 x 43.2 cm)
Cotton on collar interfacing;
appliquéd, machine sewn
Photo by Don Tuttle

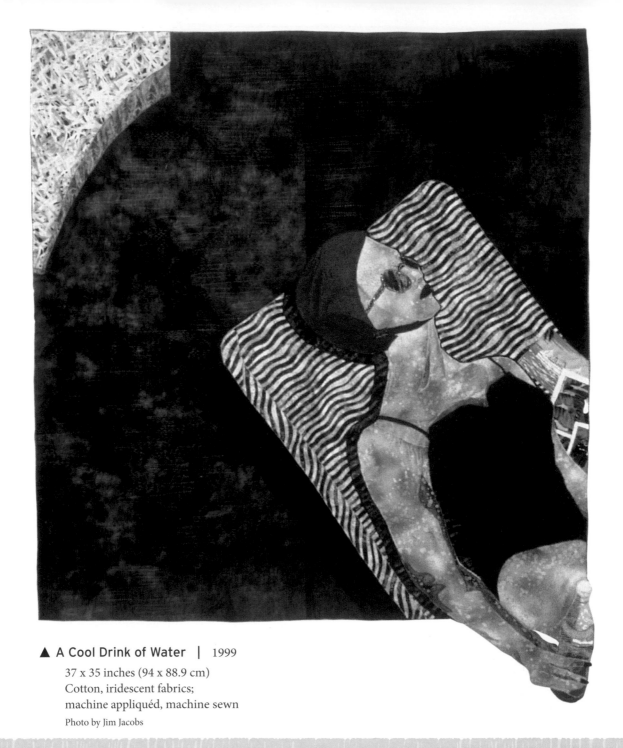

▲ A Cool Drink of Water | 1999

37 x 35 inches (94 x 88.9 cm)
Cotton, iridescent fabrics;
machine appliquéd, machine sewn

Photo by Jim Jacobs

" I incorporate
the qualities of
light, shadow, and
perspective used
by artists in other
media, but without
the use of paint
or other surface
treatments. Instead,
I produce the effects
using snippets of
fabric prints. "

Love in Bloom | 2007 ▶
29 x 19½ inches (73.7 x 49.5 cm)
Cotton on collar interfacing;
appliquéd, machine sewn
Photo by Don Tuttle

Beatrice Lanter

HUNDREDS OF TINY FABRIC PIECES create a joyful dance of color and light in the work of Beatrice Lanter. Inspired by the natural beauty of her native Switzerland, Lanter's palette often includes greens, blues, and pinks. Many of her pieces feature tiny machine-pieced and quilted log cabin blocks, some pieced traditionally and some reversed so that the seams show and the fabric edges unravel.

The harmony and dissonance of the colors used in each slightly asymmetrical block create an interplay of sparkling light. A frequent experimenter, Lanter likes to highlight the visual tension that occurs when structured, traditional blocks are contrasted with a free-form color placement.

Reflecting her explorations of the interaction between color and transparency, Lanter's recent quilts incorporate translucent organza ribbons, which she accents with French knots or appliquéd butterfly shapes. Some of these pieces depart completely from the traditional rectangular quilt form to become strings of vines or floating feathers. Delicate and fragile-looking, these organza creations nonetheless evoke Lanter's delight in the explosive growth and energy of gardens in spring.

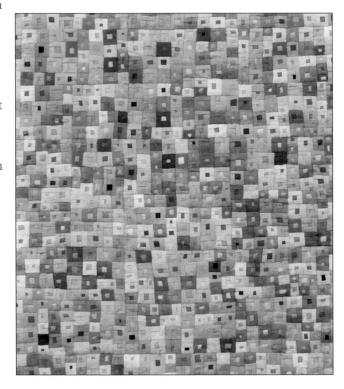

▲ Vergnügt | 2009

43⁵/₁₆ x 43⁵/₁₆ inches (110 x 110 cm)
Cotton, linen; hand dyed, machine sewn,
hand knotted

Photos by artist

◄ Freude | 2004
33⅞ x 33½ inches (86 x 85 cm)
Cotton, linen; hand dyed,
machine sewn, hand knotted
Photo by artist

" Color and structure are important to me.

I like painting with small pieces of fabric. "

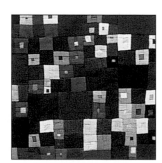

Lights | 2001 ►
48½ x 57½ inches (1.2 x 1.5 m)
Cotton; machine pieced,
hand quilted
Photos by artist

▲ Wiese | 2007

 41¾ x 41¾ inches (106 x 106 cm)
 Cotton, linen; hand dyed, machine sewn,
 hand knotted

 Photo by artist

▲ Hinten II | 2007

40^{15}/$_{16}$ x 40^{15}/$_{16}$ inches (104 x 104 cm)
Cotton, linen; hand dyed, machine sewn,
machine quilted

Photo by artist

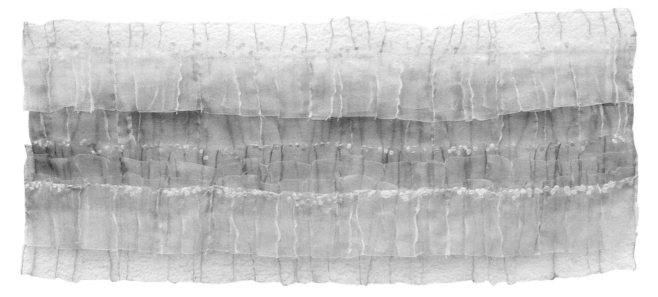

▲ Garten I | 2008
   11¹/₁₆ x 25⁵/₈ inches (28 x 65 cm)
   Polyester-organza ribbons;
   machine sewn, machine embroidered
   Photo by artist

Garten II | 2008 ▶
   25⁵/₈ x 18¹⁵/₁₆ inches (65 x 48 cm)
   Polyester-organza ribbons;
   machine sewn, machine
   embroidered
   Photo by artist

BEATRICE LANTER

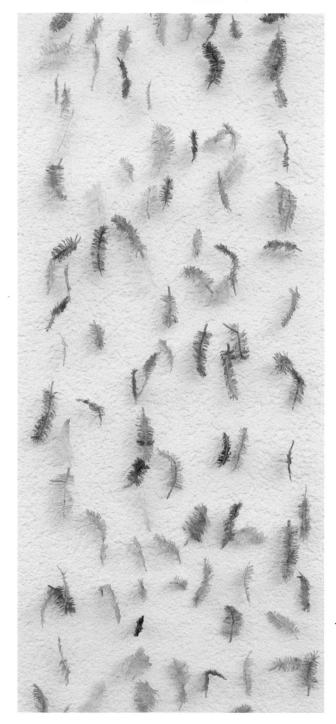

LANTER

BEATRICE

" Some time ago I discovered
that a piece often looks more
interesting on the reverse
than on the front. I became
more and more interested
in the reverse. Now, for me,
there's no longer any back or
front to a piece. There's no
right and no wrong. "

◀ Fliegen II | 2009

80¾ x 17¾ inches (2 x 0.4 m)
Polyester organza; machine
embroidered, hand painted,
hand sewn

Photo by artist

▲ Wachsen | 2006

40½ x 41 inches (103 x 104 cm)
Cotton, linen; hand dyed,
machine sewn, knotted

Photo by artist

◀ Geschenk | 2002

23⅝ x 23⅝ inches (60 x 60 cm)
Polyester-organza ribbons, cotton;
hand sewn

Photo by artist

" Two parts of my creative life come
together in my quilts: Drawing, of which
I'm very fond, is now part of my textile
work. I draw with the sewing machine. "

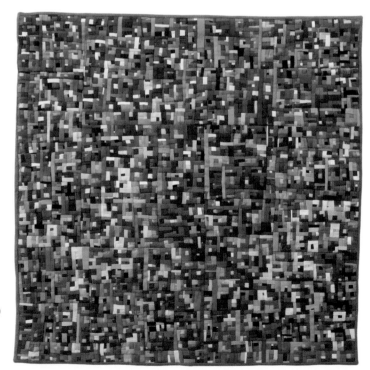

Unkraut | 2005 ▶

29⁹⁄₁₆ x 28¾ inches (75 x 73 cm)
Cotton, linen; hand dyed,
machine sewn, hand knotted

Photo by artist

▲ Hinten III | 2008

34¹¹/₁₆ x 31⁷/₈ inches (88 x 81 cm)
Cotton, linen; hand dyed, machine sewn,
machine quilted

Photo by artist

Tafi Brown

LONG BEFORE PHOTOGRAPHS could be manipulated by computer, Tafi Brown was creating kaleidoscopic patterns from cyanotype prints of photos on fabric. Beginning with an art quilt that commemorated the construction of her timber-frame home in New Hampshire, Brown has employed the same process for more than 30 years. She uses chemical formulas that were developed in the 1840s, which produce deep Prussian and cobalt blues that don't fade.

She combines Kodalith negatives made from her own photographs with fabrics printed using photograms—sun prints created with pine needles, flowers, and other natural items. In Brown's quilts, the photo repeats are mirrored and pieced together, producing variations in color and a richness of tone that aren't possible with computer-manipulated images.

Featuring photos from her everyday life or from her travels to Japan and the Galapagos, Brown's tantalizing work plays with visual ambiguity. She often highlights the unexpected in her designs by hiding items under flaps of fabric. Perhaps the biggest surprise for viewers comes when they realize the lacy kaleidoscopic patterns they see are made up of repeats of photos—images of construction equipment, cityscapes, and body parts.

Ifilwami: The Dream | 2006 ▶

62 x 44 inches (1.5 x 1.1 m)
Cotton, cyanotype photographs;
machine pieced, machine quilted
Photos by Jeff Baird

▲ **Logs** | 1994

21 x 21 inches (53.3 x 53.3 cm)
Cotton, cyanotype prints; machine embroidered,
machine appliquéd, machine sewn, machine quilted

Photo by artist

" I love quilting
because it's a
user-friendly
art form, and
people of all ages
can relate to it.
My art almost
always sparks a
conversation. "

▲ Joint Effort | 1993

62 x 62 inches (1.5 x 1.5 m)
Cotton, commercial fabrics, cyanotype photographs and photograms;
hand dyed, airbrushed, machine appliquéd, machine quilted
Photo by Jeff Nintzel

▲ **Aizu–Wakamatsu** | 2000

34 x 44 inches (86.4 x 111.8 cm)
Cotton, cyanotype photographs;
machine pieced, machine quilted
Photo by Jeff Baird

" I develop each quilt in the same way that a painter paints a picture. I execute the entire piece on a wall, adding parts and pieces or taking them away and moving things around until the quilt works as a whole. "

▲ Sengakuji Temple Gables | 2000

44 x 44 inches (111.8 x 111.8 cm)
Cotton, cyanotype photographs; hand dyed

Photos by Jeff Baird

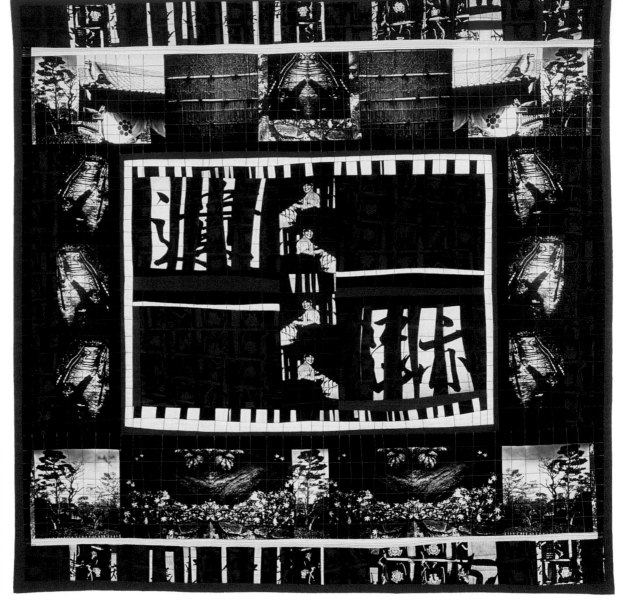

▲ Aizu–Wakamatsu: Matsunaga | 2000

39 x 39 inches (99.1 x 99.1 cm)
Cotton, cyanotype photographs; machine pieced,
machine quilted

Photos by Jeff Baird

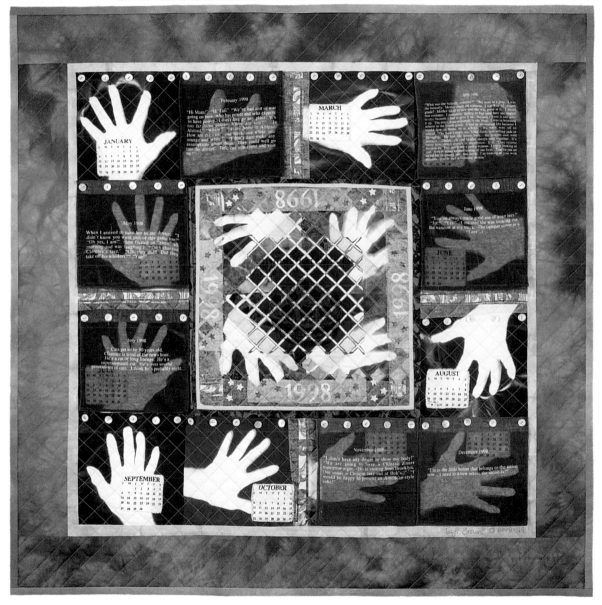

▲ **OMOM!** | 1999

42 x 41 inches (106.7 x 104.1 cm)
Cotton, cotton gauze, muslin dish towel, rayon ribbon, mother-of-pearl buttons,
rayon embroidery thread, cyanotype photograms; hand dyed, machine embroidered,
double stitched, reverse appliquéd, machine pieced, machine quilted
Photo by Jeff Baird

" Quilting feeds
my love of fabrics
and texture. It
also satisfies my
need to be a part
of the continuum
of history and
to connect with
people. "

◀ **Asakusa** | 2000

58 x 41 inches (1.5 x 1.1 m)
Cotton, cyanotype photographs,
rayon piping and ribbon;
machine embroidered, machine
appliquéd, machine pieced,
machine quilted

Photo by Jeff Baird

TAFI **BROWN**

Risë Nagin

FIBER ART IS OFTEN EVALUATED in terms of elements like texture, stitch, color, and form. Risë Nagin's work adds light to that list of elements. Nagin thinks of light as a physical material; it's an essential component that she considers as she designs. Through the staining and layering of sheer fabrics, she adds levels of translucency to her compositions, creating unique visual effects that change depending on the viewer's perspective.

Though she considers herself a painter, Nagin works with fabric because it conducts light in ways that paint can't. Led by intuition, she experiments with doodles and colored paper collages in a search for a rhythmic flow of forms.

Nagin's early quilts probe different aspects of the human experience, from impressions of a highway journey to dreamscapes populated with menacing archetypal images. Recent quilts explore ancient alchemical and sacred symbols, the meanings of which may have been lost in modern times. Other pieces are inspired by nature—the play of reflections across the surface of a lake, or scenes from an early morning walk.

Whatever her source, in each of her quilts Nagin evokes a lyrical experience of beauty.

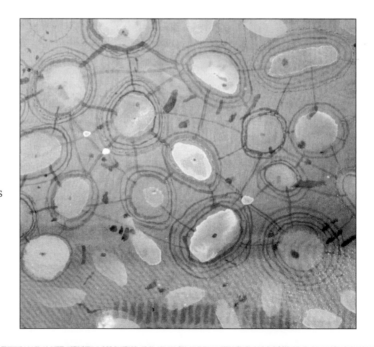

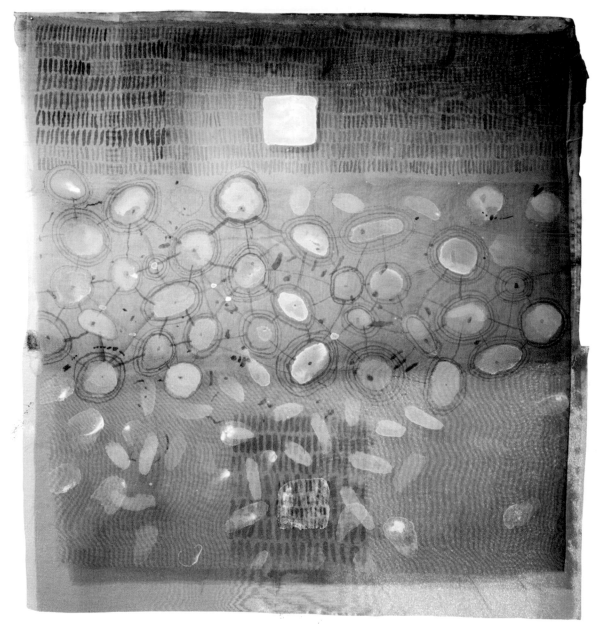

▲ Illumination | 2004

17 x 16 inches (43.2 x 40.6 cm)
Silk, nylon, polyester, gouache, acrylic paint, thread;
layered, appliquéd, embroidered, quilted, hand sewn
Photos by Larry Rippel

▲ Road Goliaths | 1985

56¾ x 70½ inches (1.4 x 1.7 m)
Silk, polyester, cotton, acetate, acrylic paint, thread;
stained, layered, appliquéd, pieced, embroidered,
hand sewn, machine constructed

Photo by Sam Newbury

▲ Target: On the Beach | 1993

80 x 99¼ inches (2 x 2.5 m)
Silk, cotton, polyester, acrylic paint, thread;
stained, layered, pieced, appliquéd, quilted, hand sewn

Photo by artist

▲ Three Sisters | 1992

72 x 94 inches (1.8 x 2.3 m)
Silk, cotton, polyester, acrylic paint, thread; stained,
layered, pieced, appliquéd, quilted, hand sewn
Photo by artist

▲ Confection | 2006

12 x 12 inches (30.5 x 30.5 cm)
Silk, acrylic, gouache, textile paint, thread;
layered, appliquéd, quilted, hand sewn

Photo by Martha Wasik

" My quilts are directly related to my painting practice. I try to exploit the qualities of

textiles in order to achieve images that are akin in impact and ideas to painting. "

▲ Gate | 1989

  70 x 70 inches (1.7 x 1.7 m)
  Silk, cotton, polyester, felt, acrylic paint, cellophane, thread;
  stained, layered, pieced, appliquéd, embroidered, quilted, hand sewn
  Photo by Lockwood Hoehl

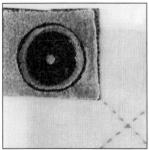

▲ **Codex: Mandala + Cross–Installation** | 2006

Overall: 50 x 94 inches (1.2 x 2.3 m)
Silk, polyester, fusible interfacing, gouache,
thread; appliquéd, quilted, hand sewn

Sewing assistant: Barbara Rice
Main photo by Larry Rippel
Detail photo by John Clines

" Cloth conducts light in singular ways that I manipulate to create

luminosity and a sense of atmosphere in my work. "

RISË NAGIN

▲ Heliotaxis | 2006

138 x 420 inches (3.5 x 10.6 m)
Silk, polyester, cotton, gouache, acrylic paint,
thread, bonding agents; stained, appliquéd,
embroidered, layered, bonded, hand sewn

Photos by Larry Rippel

Maquette | 2006 ▶

77 x 71 inches (1.9 x 1.8 m)
Silk, polyester, cotton, gouache,
acrylic paint, thread; stained,
layered, appliquéd, quilted,
hand sewn and fused

Photo by John Clines

RISË **NAGIN**

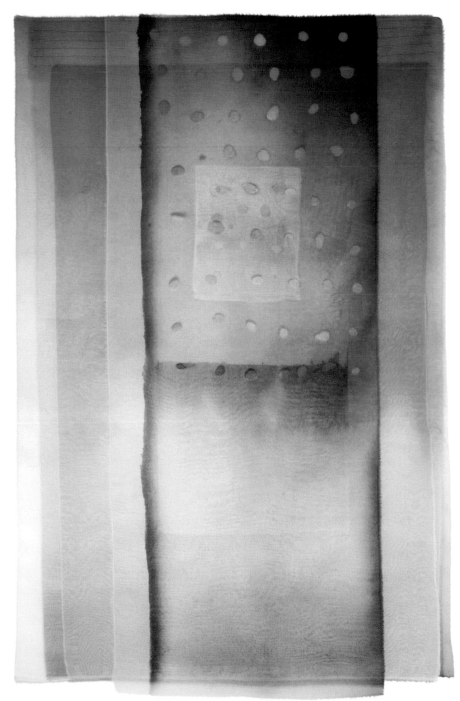

" I want my work to reflect the intimate, ancient connection that exists between maker and object. "

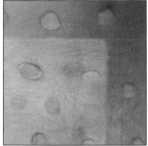

◀ Union | 2001

49 x 32 inches (124.5 x 81.3 cm)
Silk, nylon, fabric dyes, acrylic paint, thread; stained, burned, layered, appliquéd, embroidered, quilted, hand sewn

Photos by Larry Rippel

RISË NAGIN

Bente Vold Klausen

THE MEDIA IS FULL OF VIOLENT IMAGES that can create an overwhelming sense of menace. This ominous quality pervades much of Bente Vold Klausen's work. Sometimes the sense of unease is based upon events reported in the news. Sometimes Klausen invents her own scenarios—crime stories that lend interest to a work. Inspired also by a variety of other influences—folk art, the landscape of her native Norway, or environmental issues—she lets her intuition guide her as she creates a personal vocabulary of symbols, words, and geometric forms.

Primarily made out of whole cloth, Klausen's quilts feature a variety of techniques, including dyeing, painting, and printing. She uses these methods to create layer upon layer of imagery, which she then machine quilts. Frequent designs include simplified human forms, spirals, windows, and scattered triangles or dots. Two of her most intriguing motifs are targets and hands. The hands are usually helping, hugging, or reaching out for connection, while the targets clearly signify danger.

Klausen's works may be playful or poignant, but—regardless of mood—they all powerfully communicate her sense of urgency about contemporary issues.

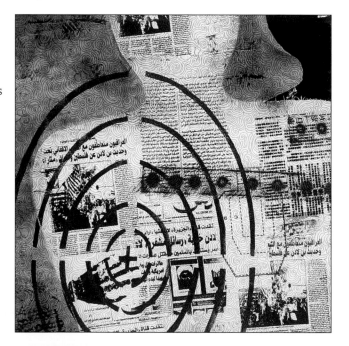

Hunted 4 | 2006 ▶

67³⁄₁₆ x 48 inches (1.7 x 1.2 m)
Cotton; hand dyed, printed,
painted, screen-printed,
machine quilted

Photos by artist

" I enjoy working without a great deal of planning—fast and with a lot of physical motion. As a result, my latest pieces seem like paintings. **"**

▲ **Crime Scene** | 2004

62$\frac{1}{16}$ x 50$\frac{3}{8}$ inches (1.6 x 1.6 m)
Cotton; hand dyed, printed, painted, machine quilted

Photo by artist

Princess in Mountain Blue | 2004 ▶

55 x 49 inches (1.4 x 1.26 m)
Cotton, textile paint; hand dyed,
printed, machine quilted

Photo by artist

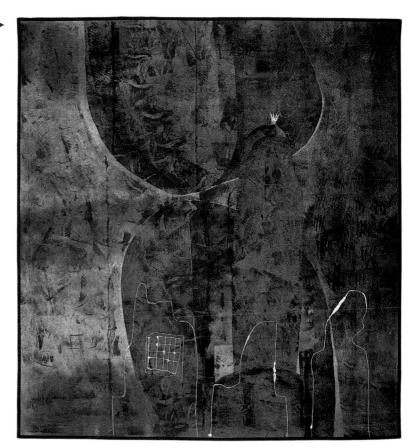

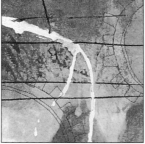

◀ **Once Upon a Time** | 2004

77 x 62 inches (1.9 x 1.5 m)
Cotton, textile paint; hand dyed,
printed, machine quilted

Photos by artist

" I take a lot of photos, because I'm fascinated by details, textures, and surfaces. A photo will often provide me with the basic inspiration for a piece. "

KLAUSEN

Forfedre (Ancestors) | 2004 ▶
19 x 26 inches (48 x 68 cm)
Cotton, textile paint; hand dyed,
printed, machine quilted
Photo by artist

Hunted | 2006 ▶

62⅞ x 54⁵/₁₆ inches (1.6 x 1.4 m)
Cotton; hand dyed, printed,
painted, machine quilted

Photos by artist

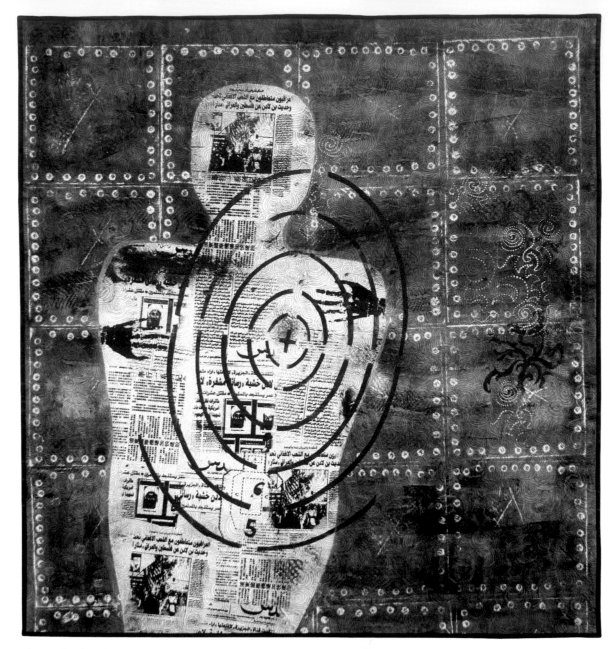

▲ Hunted 2 | 2006

53⅛ x 50⅜ inches (1.3 x 1.3 m)
Cotton; hand dyed, printed, painted, machine quilted
Photo by artist

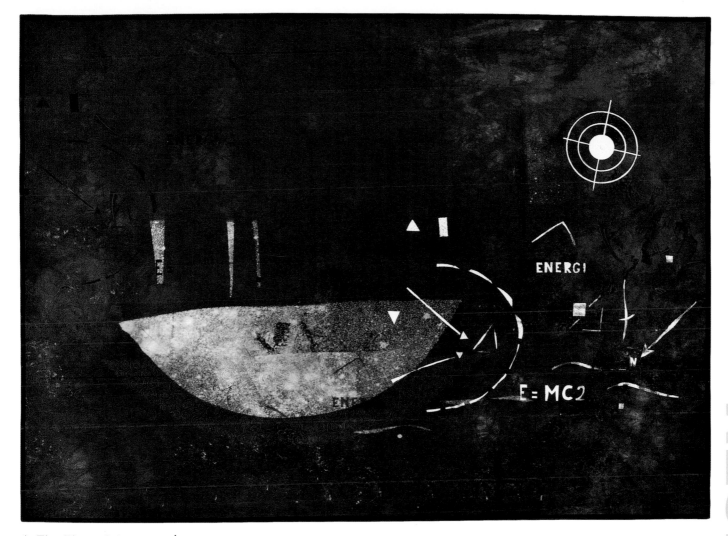

▲ The Eternal Journey | 2008

41¾ x 57⅜ inches (1 x 1.4 m)
Cotton; hand dyed, printed, painted,
discharged, machine quilted

Photo by artist

" The sewing machine has been my favorite tool since childhood. I love free-motion quilting, and I'm forever experimenting with threads, seams, and patterns. "

▲ **Eternal Energy** | 2008

41¾ x 56¹/₁₆ inches (1 x 1.4 m)
Cotton; hand dyed, printed, painted,
discharged, machine quilted

Photo by artist

▲ Dreams on Fire | 2008

41⅝/₁₆ x 55⅞ inches (1 x 1.4 m)
Cotton; hand dyed, printed, painted,
discharged, machine quilted

Photo by artist

Jane Dunnewold

AT FIRST GLANCE, THE VIBRANT QUILTS made by Jane Dunnewold seem to be all about the array of surface design techniques she layers and combines in each length of what is known as "complex cloth." But Dunnewold's work also thoughtfully explores deep messages about family, motherhood, and the earth's fragility.

Dunnewold has said that her goal is to create cloth that sings. She succeeds thanks to the use of rich patterns, which she creates through dye resists, screen-printing, lamination, devore, and digital manipulation—techniques that create rhythmic underpinnings in her cloth.

Made of two layers, with tops that are often fused to industrial felt, Dunnewold's quilts feature striking focal elements, which can include animals, flowers, and children. She uses hand stitching and needle felting to quilt the layers, but the stitch and its line are secondary to the overall design of the whole cloth surface.

Dunnewold savors the long, slow process of creating multiple layers of dye and paint. Taking her time allows her to explore the visual surfaces and reflect upon how the interplay of their patterned layers is a means to investigate their spiritual messages.

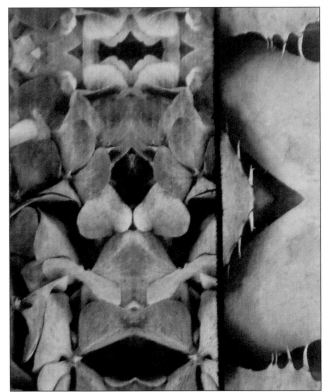

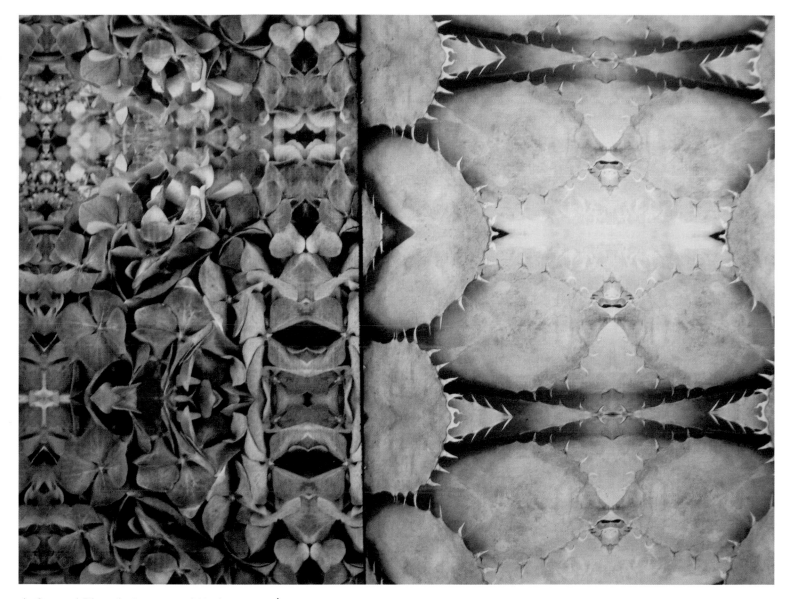

▲ **Sacred Planet: Agave and Hydrangea** | 2009

48 x 55 inches (1.2 x 1.4 m)
Cotton fabric, industrial felt, gold leaf, digital photos:
assembled, fused, machine stitched

Digital photos printed by spoonflower.com
Photos by artist

▲ **Wartime Prayer for the Children and the Flowers** | 2008

72 x 60 inches (1.8 x 1.5 m)

Cotton lawn, industrial felt; dyed, soy-wax resist, discharged, body prints, screen-printed, hand colored, dyed, hand stitched, machine stitched

Photo by artist

" I like playing with different kinds of stitches. Knots, straight stitches, revamped embroidery stitches—all are fair game and often replace a more traditional stitched line. "

▲ Baby Quilt | 1994

48 x 44 inches (121.9 x 111.8 cm)
Cotton, silk, birthday candles, polyester binding,
photo transfers; burned, machine quilted

Text from *The Prophet* by Kahlil Gibran
Photos by artist

▲ Growth III | 2009
   60 x 45 inches (1.5 x 1.1 m)
   Silk habotai, cotton lawn, industrial
   felt; dyed, soy-wax resist, discharged,
   hand drawn, watercolor, devore,
   machine stitched
   Photo by artist

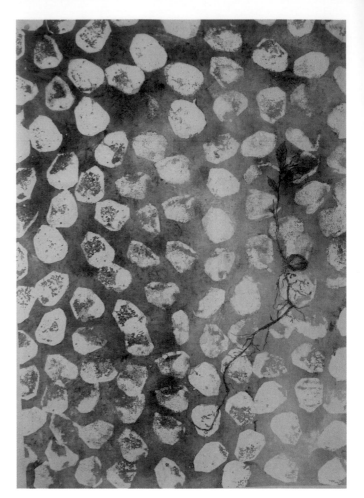

▲ Growth I | 2008
   38 x 28 inches (96.5 x 71.1 cm)
   Cotton lawn, industrial felt, polyester web,
   wool batting, perle cotton; soy-wax resist,
   faux-gel resist, dyed, discharged, hand drawn,
   hand colored, needle felted, hand stitched
   Photo by artist

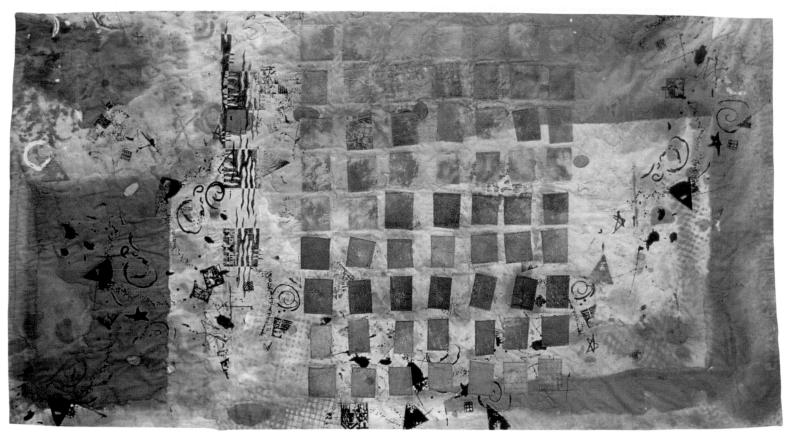

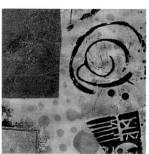

▲ Seeking Order | 1996

45 x 84 inches (1.1 x 2.1 m)
Cotton, puff paint, paper; hand painted,
screen-printed, machine quilted

Photos by artist

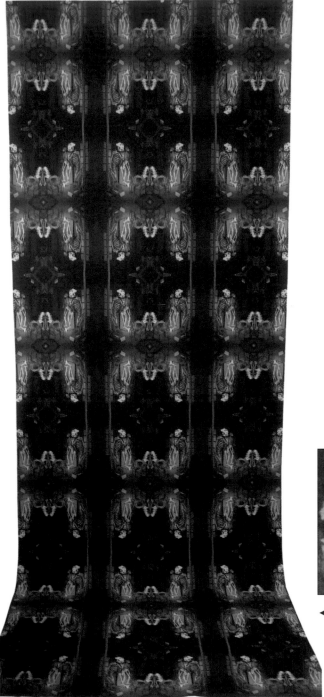

" I gave up middle batting a few years ago. I prefer the flat, almost architectural surface I get when I fuse my heavily layered top fabric to industrial felt. The surface is smooth, but there's enough depth to allow the stitched marks to either disappear or contribute based on the look I want. "

◄ **Sacred Planet: The Illusion of Human Superiority** | 2009

108 x 40 inches (2.7 x 1 m)

Cotton fabric, industrial felt, gold leaf, digital photos; assembled, fused, machine stitched, screen-printed with black sand

Digital photos printed by spoonflower.com

Photos by artist

▲ Pear | 1998

54 x 54 inches (1.3 x 1.3 m)
Cotton, puff paint, batting; hand painted,
silk-screened, machine quilted

Photo by artist

▲ **Fortitude of Motherhood** | 1992

54 x 48 inches (137.1 x 121.9 cm)
Cotton, batting, straight pins, photo transfers;
machine quilted

Photo by artist

" It takes time to figure out what works with digital imagery in a piece. Adding a sand print—a gel base covered with black sand that dries to produce a complete, raised image— often creates an effect that I like when combined with photography. "

◀ **Sacred Planet: Storks** | 2009

108 x 40 inches (2.7 x 1 m)
Cotton fabric, industrial felt, gold leaf, digital photos; assembled, fused, machine stitched, screen-printed with black sand

Digital photos printed by spoonflower.com
Photos by artist

JANE DUNNEWOLD

Laura Wasilowski

CONJURING A DELIGHTFULLY QUIRKY WORLD that's a bit off kilter, the quilts made by Laura Wasilowski will brighten any viewer's day. Her works are made from fabrics she hand dyes in bright colors then cuts and fuses into pieces that commemorate the joys of everyday life. Her signature hues include bright greens, turquoises, and oranges, and she favors small circles, stripes, and brick patterns—shapes that often fill her surfaces. To add emphasis, she machine quilts and embroiders by hand.

Wasilowski is a storyteller who likes to explore certain themes repeatedly in her work. She calls herself a "serial quilter." The daughter of an Illinois farmer, she reminisces about her childhood in pieces that chronicle nature's cycle of growth and rebirth. The whimsical, tipsy houses that appear in her quilts represent friends and family, while her "kitchenscapes"—colorful depictions of chairs, chickens, dogs, and teapots—celebrate the commonplace.

Wasilowski also creates pieces that pay homage to the tools of her trade: paintbrushes, scissors, and, of course, irons. In addition to skill and craftsmanship, her quilts reflect a wry sense of humor and a taste for narrative.

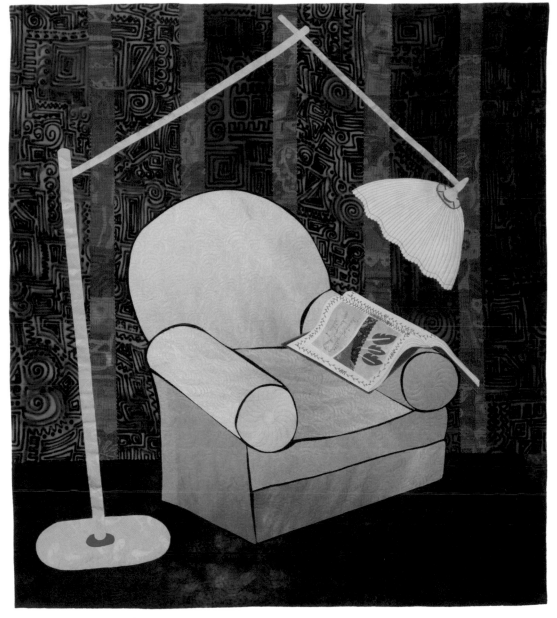

▲ Reading Lamp | 2009

44 x 40 inches (111.8 x 101.6 cm)
Silk, fusible appliqué; hand dyed,
machine quilted

Photos by George Tarbay

▲ Lacking Gravity | 2009

41 x 37 inches (1 x 0.9 m)
Cotton, fusible appliqué; hand dyed,
hand embroidered, machine quilted

Photo by George Tarbay

" Fabric scraps
are like starter
dough. The
possibilities
are endless. "

▲ Blue Ladder | 1998
52 x 41 inches (1.3 x 1 m)
Cotton, fusible appliqué; hand dyed, machine quilted
Photos by George Tarbay

LAURA **WASILOWSKI**

▼ Red Wheelbarrow | 1998

46 x 41 inches (116.8 x 104.1 cm)
Cotton, fusible appliqué;
hand dyed, machine quilted

Photos by George Tarbay

▲ Penelope's Peaches | 2002

35 x 34 inches (88.9 x 86.4 cm)
Cotton, fusible appliqué;
hand dyed, machine quilted

Photo by George Tarbay

" Everyday tasks
and objects
inspire my
quilt designs.
I have a deep
appreciation for
the ordinary. "

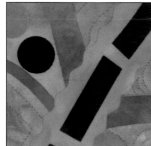

▲ **Leaf Motif** | 2009
45 x 41 inches (1.1 x 1 m)
Cotton, fusible appliqué; hand dyed, machine quilted
Photos by George Tarbay

LAURA WASILOWSKI

▲ Fences and Bridges #2 | 2008

35 x 29 inches (88.9 x 73.6 cm)
Cotton, fusible appliqué; hand dyed, machine quilted

Photos by George Tarbay

LAURA WASILOWSKI

" Creating art in an improvisational manner is a joyful act. Without any planning, I can entertain myself for hours by clipping fabric, ironing shapes into place, and making compositions from leftover material. "

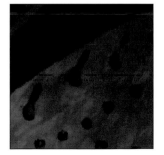

▲ Ironic Conclusions | 1996

53 x 45 inches (1.3 x 1.1 m)
Cotton, fusible appliqué; hand dyed, machine quilted
Photos by George Tarbay

▲ **Farm** | 1998

55 x 51 inches (1.4 x 1.3 m)
Cotton, fusible appliqué; hand dyed,
stamped, machine quilted

Photos by George Tarbay

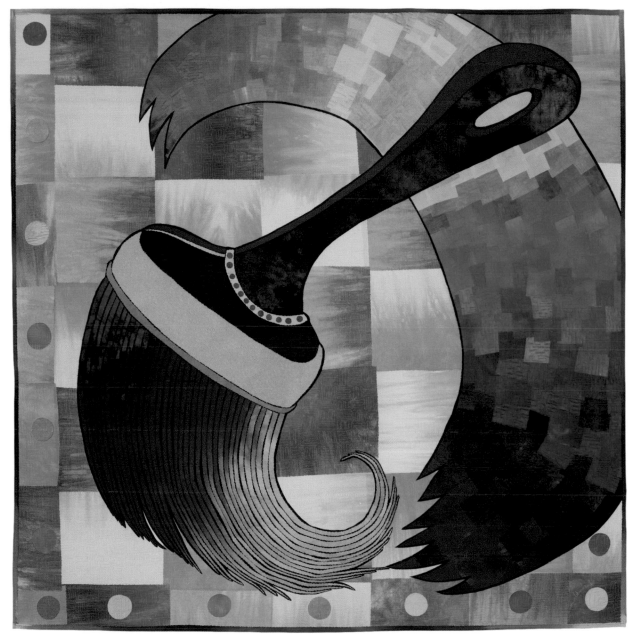

▲ **Artfabrik** | 2004

51 x 51 inches (1.3 x 1.3 m)
Cotton, silk, fusible appliqué; hand dyed, machine quilted
Photo by George Tarbay

Arturo Alonzo Sandoval

INNOVATIVE WORKS THAT PUSH the boundaries of the medium, Arturo Alonzo Sandoval's art quilts feature modern materials and nontraditional techniques. Sandoval's goal is to create beauty from the residue of modern culture—an aesthetic decision that's reflected in his choice of materials. Over the years, he has made work from Army surplus supplies, discarded microfilm, and painting canvases abandoned by his students at the University of Kentucky at Louisville.

Sandoval constructs each quilt from layers of plastics such as vinyl and Mylar, which he connects with zigzag stitches of varying sizes that add an extra graphic element to the work. Instead of piecing or appliquéing the layers, he interlaces them. He enjoys experimenting with form and often makes three-dimensional pieces that revolve. He believes the interior of a quilt should be as aesthetically engaging as the surface. By using transparent materials, he's able to make every part of a piece visible to viewers.

Always original and inventive, Sandoval is a pioneer. For the viewer, his groundbreaking quilts are simply works of wonder.

▲ Millennium Portal No. 2 | 2000

72 inches (1.8 m) in diameter
Plastic, recycled paintings on canvas, netting, color threads,
Cibachromes, heat press tape, polymer medium, hook-and-loop
tape; interlaced, machine stitched and embroidered
Photos by Tim Collins

▲ Cosmic Spiral No. 2 | 2003
7½ x 7¼ feet (2.3 x 2.2 m)
Plastic sheeting, leader film, microfilm, canvas, paint, netting,
colored and monofilament threads, polymer adhesive,
hook-and-loop tape; interlaced, machine stitched
Photo by Tim Collins

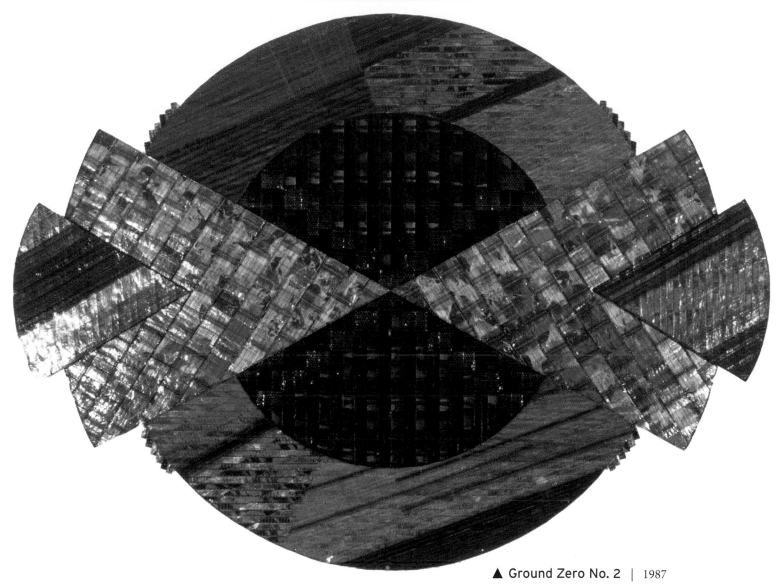

▲ **Ground Zero No. 2** | 1987

52½ x 71½ inches (1.3 x 1.8 m)
Film, acetate copies, paint, plastic,
bleached movie film, netting,
photo-screened vinyl, eyelets; machine
stitched, embroidered, interlaced

Photo by Mary S. Rezny

" I listen to my materials, and I play with them. I try to express

what they're saying visually, to be guided by what they tell me. "

▲ Millennium | 1998

20¼ x 40 x 1½ feet (6.1 x 12.1 x 0.4 m)
Modular panels, fire-retardant canvas, plastic sheeting, recycled roll-leaf tape, millinery netting, polyester/rayon threads, monofilament thread, polymer adhesive, hook-and-loop tape, spray paint, donated yarns and metallic threads, motorized modular steel mounts; compression resist, machine stitched and embroidered

Photos by Tim Collins

" The use of exotic materials and high-tech products gives my pieces a unique aesthetic. Thanks to these materials, the reflections emitted by the surfaces of my forms lend an added dimension to the work. "

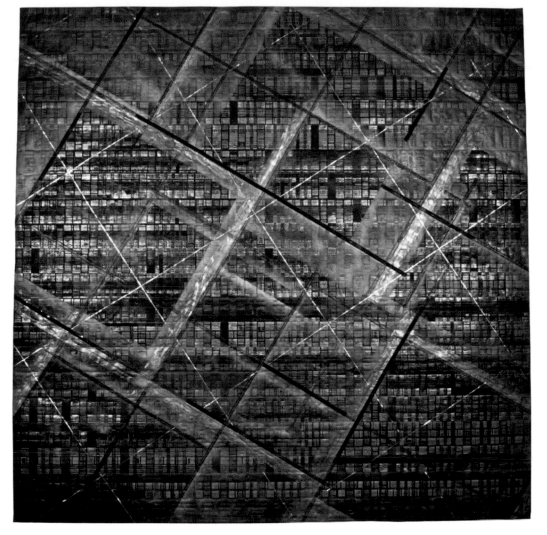

▲ Cityscape No. 7 | 1978

84 x 84 inches (2.1 x 2.1 m)
Microfilm, laundry tag paper, plastic
sheeting, metallic yarn, paint, eyelets;
machine stitched and interlaced

Photo by Mary S. Rezny

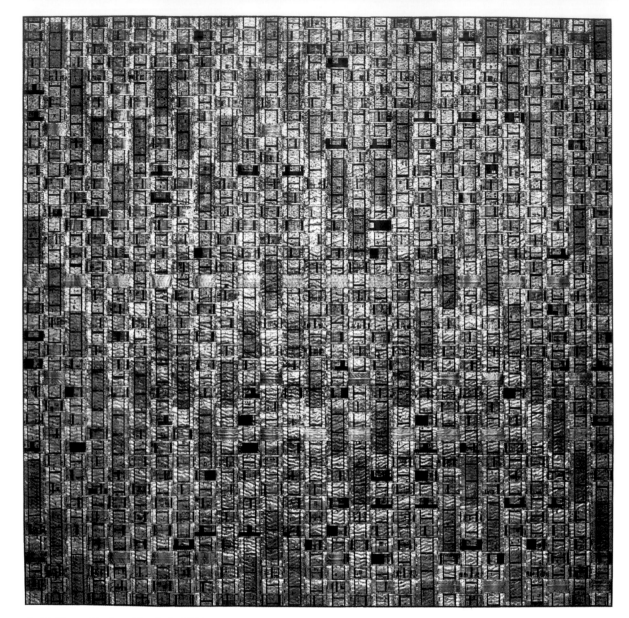

▲ **Pattern Fusion No. 1** | 2004

60½ x 60½ inches (1.5 x 1.5. m)
Recycled auto-industry plastic, recycled library microfilm,
netting, monofilament and multi-colored threads, plaited braid,
polymer medium; machine stitched and interlaced

Photo by Tim Collins

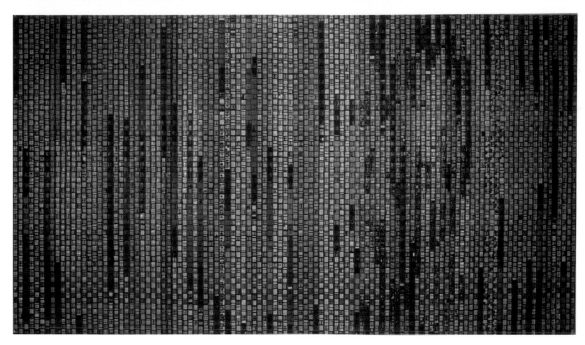

▲ Cityscape No. 5 | 1978

84 x 151 inches (2.1 x 3.8 m)
Microfilm, laundry tag paper,
plastic sheeting, hook-and-loop tape;
machine stitched and interlaced

Photo by Mary S. Rezny

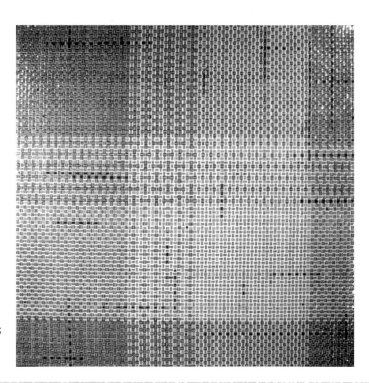

Cityscape No. 1 | 1977 ▶

84 x 84 inches (2.1 x 2.1 m)
Microfilm, laundry tag paper,
plastic sheeting, metallic yarn,
cotton edging, hook-and-loop tape;
machine stitched and interlaced

Photo by Mary S. Rezny

ARTURO ALONZO SANDOVAL

▲ ¡Guerra! | 1993

58½ x 97 x 1 inches (1.4 x 2.4 x 0.2 m)
Flag, fabric, netting, paint, plastic skeletons, cloth letters,
colored and monofilament threads, nylon rope, rayon, fringe,
eyelets; hand and machine stitched

Photo by Mary S. Rezny

" Systems of weaving and interlacing have always been important to me creatively.

Through weaving, I can express myself and add meaning to a work. "

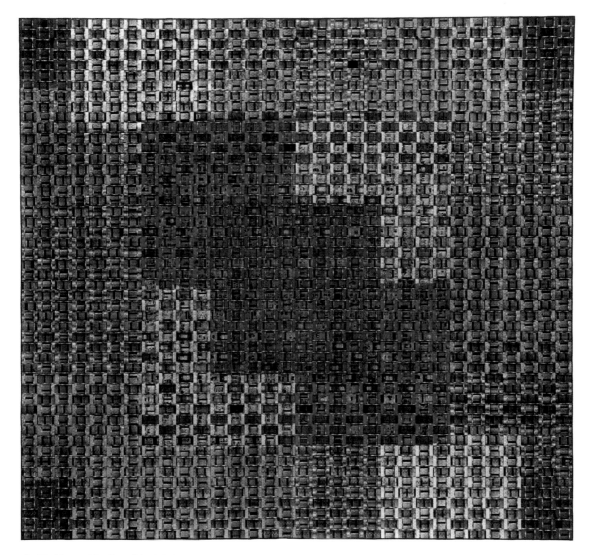

▲ **Pattern Fusion No. 7** | 2006

73¼ x 69 inches (1.8 x 1.7 m)
Recycled auto-industry plastic, recycled library microfilm,
netting, multi-colored threads, plaited braid, polymer medium;
machine stitched and interlaced

Photo by Tim Collins

Izabella Baykova

CAPTURING THE MAGICAL PLAY OF LIGHT in snow, smoke, and mist, Izabella Baykova blends fantasy and reality in her exquisite quilts. The Russian cityscapes and fairy tales she depicts are inspired by the view from her apartment building in St. Petersburg and by classic folk stories. Her background as a professionally trained muralist and stained-glass artist translates easily into a style that features pieced backgrounds with details created through satin-stitched appliqué and embroidery.

Baykova makes use of the texture and translucency of many different textiles, but she works primarily with layers of sheer silk, painting the fabric in order to create the desired mood and effect. Some of her pieces include a column of color swatches placed a little to the side of the main image. This element breaks the picture plane and makes the viewer aware of the artist's guiding hand. Otherwise, one could easily become lost, immersed in Baykova's incredibly detailed scenes and the stories she tells through real and imaginary characters.

▲ **Little Night Serenade # 13 Allegro** | 2007

74 x 90 inches (1.8 x 2.3 m)

Silk; appliquéd, machine sewn, hand embroidered

Photos by Andrey Zhilin

BAYKOVA
IZABELLA

The Tower | 2008 ▶
67 x 55 inches (1.7 x 1.4 m)
Silk; hand painted,
hand embroidered
Photo by Andrey Zhilin

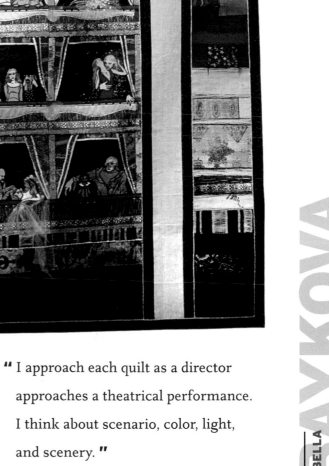

▲ **Theatre** | 2004

78 x 98 inches (1.9 x 2.5 m)
Silk, rayon; appliquéd,
machine sewn,
hand embroidered

Photos by Andrey Zhilin

" I approach each quilt as a director
approaches a theatrical performance.
I think about scenario, color, light,
and scenery. "

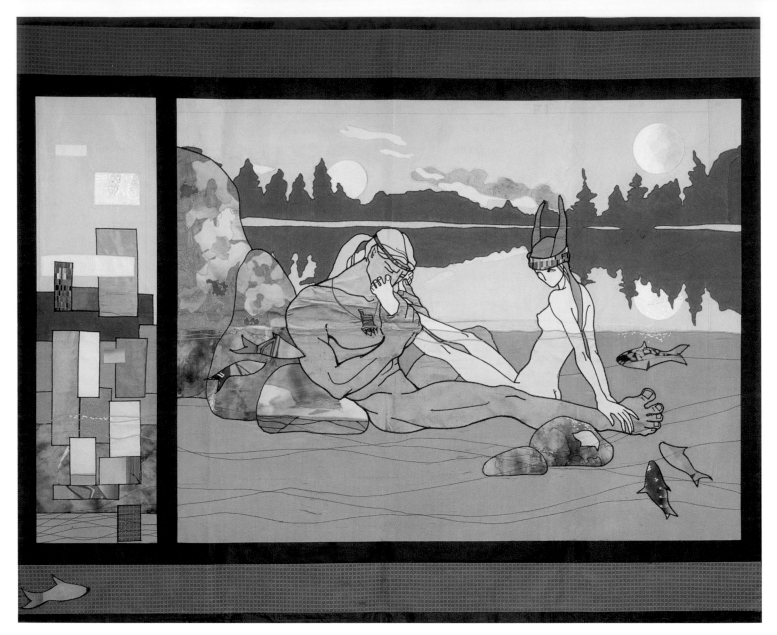

" Through my art I reconnect with my feminine side

and with the earth. Both inspire me creatively. "

▲ Bride Abduction | 2002

29 x 36 inches (75 x 93 cm)
Silk; machine sewn,
hand embroidered

Photo by Andrey Zhilin

▲ Swegurochka | 2004

62 x 63 inches (1.5 x 1.6 m)
Silk, rayon; appliquéd, machine sewn, hand embroidered
Photo by Andrey Zhilin

▲ **Frosty Morning** | 2003

41 x 42 inches (105 x 107 cm)
Silk; machine sewn, hand embroidered
Photo by Andrey Zhilin

▲ **100% Air Humidity** | 2003

45 x 56 inches (114 x 143 cm)
Silk, rayon; appliquéd, machine sewn, hand embroidered
Photo by Andrey Zhilin

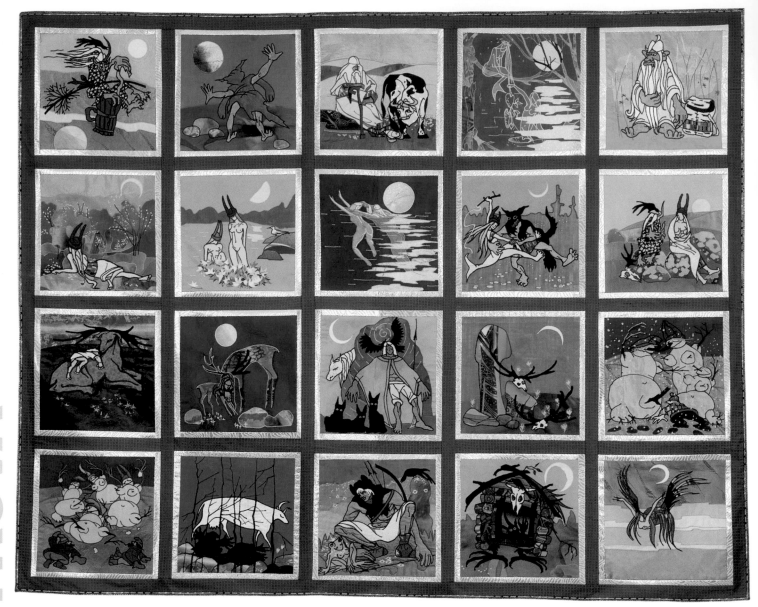

▲ Slavonic Carpet | 2002

63 x 77 inches (1.6 x 1.9 m)
Silk, rayon; appliquéd, machine sewn,
hand embroidered

Photo by Andrey Zhilin

▲ Banya | 2006

41 x 42 inches (105 x 108 cm)
Silk; appliquéd, machine sewn,
hand embroidered

Photo by Andrey Zhilin

" The construction of every quilt is like a game with the unknown. "

Daniela Dancelli

GRAFFITI ARTISTS TYPICALLY USE SPRAY PAINT to convey messages full of symbolism. Daniela Dancelli employs textiles to a similar end, designing a unique type of fiber art that feels fresh and contemporary. Dancelli's bold, abstract works combine a variety of textiles with distressed plastics, laminated newsprint, and found objects. Using thin strips of appliquéd fabric, she creates swirls of pulsating, vibrant color that resemble paint strokes. Her pieces are heavily machine quilted. Threads serve double duty, working to hold the elements of each piece together while adding rich visual detail.

Dancelli's quilts are filled with symbolic significance. Colors have special meaning: white equals innocence, black means death, and green stands for the breath of life. Representing important memories or family members, numbers have strong connotations for Dancelli and often appear in her work. She also incorporates text from newspapers and handwritten letters into her compositions, but the text is partly obscured, keeping the viewer guessing as to its meaning.

Some of Dancelli's quilts celebrate life and growth. Others memorialize world events. All offer a provocative glimpse into the artist's world.

▲ Prima l'Uovo o la Gallina | 2006

32¹¹/₁₆ x 27⅛ inches (83 x 69 cm)
Canvas, cotton, felt; iron-on painting, photo transfer,
appliquéd, machine sewn

Photos by artist

▲ T-Shirt | 2006

23⅝ x 61¼ inches (0.6 x 1.5 m)
Cotton, felt; machine quilted,
machine appliquéd,
photo transfer, dyed

Photos by artist

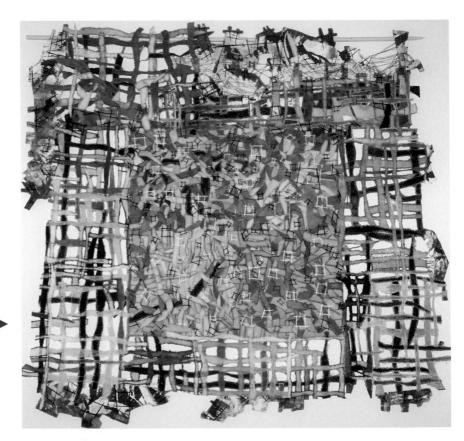

Intrecci (Interlacements) | 2007 ▶

39¾ x 39¾ inches (101 x 101 cm)
Hand-dyed cotton, soluble fabrics,
interfacing, fusible webbing,
hydrosoluble paint; machine sewn,
embroidered

Photo by artist

▲ Sognando l'America | 2008

$11^{13}/_{16}$ x $11^{13}/_{16}$ inches (30 x 30 cm)
Cotton, newspaper; hand dyed,
free-motion machine quilted,
painted, collaged

Photo by artist

" I'm fascinated by graffiti and enjoy exploring

the intersections between fiber art and street art. "

◀ Flowers | 2007

47¼ x 33⁷/₁₆ inches (120 x 85 cm)
Cotton, newspaper, glue, string;
hand dyed, free-motion machine
quilted, collaged

Photo by artist

▲ **Signs** | 2006

29½ x 35 inches (75 x 89 cm)
Cotton; hand dyed, appliquéd,
machine quilted, machine sewn

Photo by artist

" Childhood memories, family, home, and nature—

these are my main inspirations. "

▲ **Machine of Life** | 2004

51³⁄₁₆ x 51³⁄₁₆ inches (1.3 x 1.3 m)
Cotton, silk, blend fabrics, washers;
machine appliquéd, machine embellished,
machine quilted, machine pieced

Photos by artist

" I enjoy trying out different colors, playing around with unusual materials, and researching new techniques. Experimentation can result in exciting combinations. "

Me | 2009 ▶

11¹³⁄₁₆ x 8¼ inches (30 x 21 cm)
Cotton, photocopy; appliquéd,
quilted, free-motion machine
quilted, photo transfer

Photo by artist

DANIELA DANCELLI

▲ **Nameless** | 2008

35⁷⁄₁₆ x 48⁷⁄₁₆ inches (90 x 123 cm)
Cotton, string; hand dyed, machine appliquéd,
machine quilted, painted, iron-on transfer

Photos by artist

▲ 8 . . . E Tutto Ricomincia | 2009

24³⁄₈ x 28⁵⁄₁₆ inches (62 x 72 cm)
Cotton, newspaper, fusible webbing, glue, blend fabrics;
collaged, machine appliquéd, machine quilted

Photo by artist

DANIELA **DANCELLI**

Margery Goodall

IN QUILTS THAT CAN ƐVOKƐ the sparseness of the Australian landscape or the bounty of a successful harvest, Margery Goodall creates abstract symphonies of texture and line. Western Australia—Goodall's native region—conceals an abundance of life, and she captures that contradiction in works of spare design and radiant color.

Goodall crafts intricate interplays of different hues using tiny scraps of fabric that are strip-pieced into lines resembling strata, then re-cut and re-pieced into long thin rows. The careful placement of repeating colors creates a sense of movement across the surface of her work. She auditions both base fabrics and strips on her design wall before combining them into one. While she uses techniques such as overdyeing, monoprinting, and drawing with textile ink pens, her primary medium is commercial cotton fabrics. In contrast, her raw-edge pieces feature a variety of other materials, including torn paper, wool, and leather.

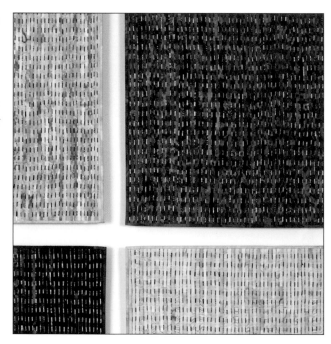

As Goodall works, she's often inspired to compose poetic verse, some of which is published to accompany the visual poetry she creates with fabric.

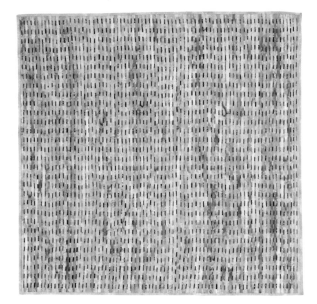

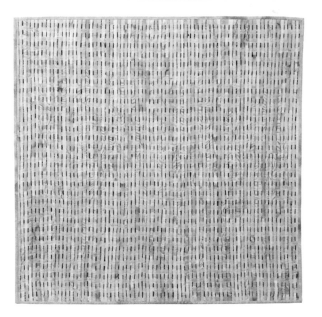

▲ Earth Suite | 2007

64¹/₁₆ x 64¹/₁₆ inches (1.6 x 1.6 m)
Commercial cottons, cotton blends, rayon, textile ink;
overdrawing, machine stitched

Photos by Beyley Shaylor

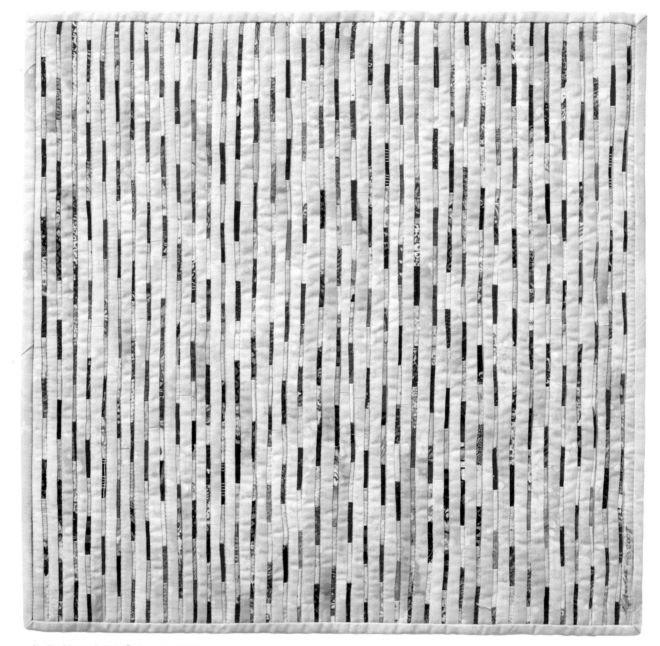

▲ Rottnest #1: Color | 2007

15¾ x 15¾ inches (40 x 40 cm)

Commercial cottons, cotton blends; machine stitched

Photo by Acorn Photo Agency

▲ **Rottnest #2: Pattern** | 2007

　　15¾ x 15¾ inches (40 x 40 cm)
　　Commercial cotton, cotton blends, rayon, textile ink;
　　overdrawing, machine stitched

　　Photo by Beyley Shaylor

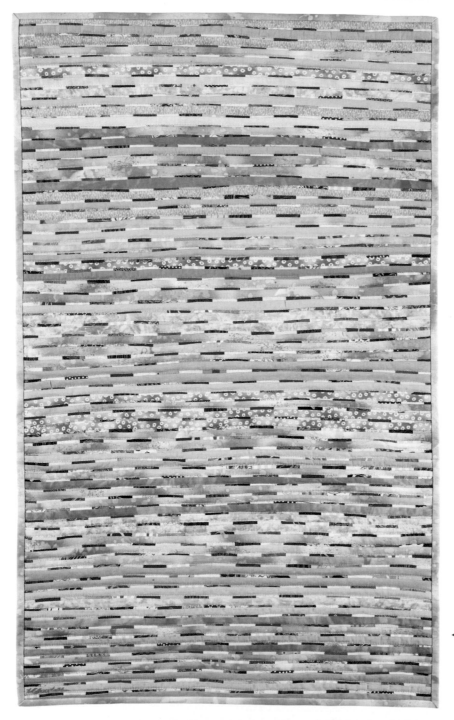

" My goal is to achieve
complexity and a quality
of the unexpected while
working with simple tools,
straightforward techniques,
and commonplace
materials. In quilt-making
terms, this is a celebration
of the ordinary. "

◀ **Summer Harvest #2** | 2002
$29^{15}/_{16}$ x $18^{7}/_{8}$ inches (76 x 48 cm)
Cotton, cotton blend, lamé blend, rayon;
machine stitched
Photo by Acorn Photo Agency

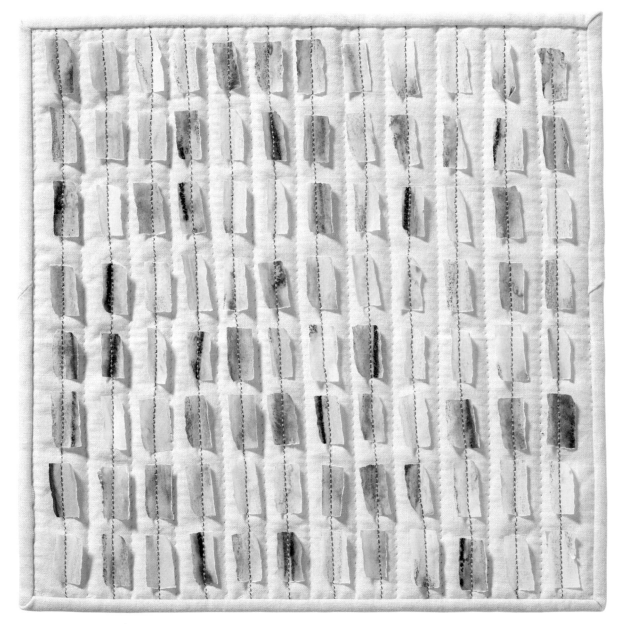

▲ **Letters Lost** | 2001

8⅝ x 8⅝ inches (22 x 22 cm)

Cotton, drafting film, watercolor paint, water-soluble pencil;
hand drawn, machine stitched

Photo by Acorn Photo Agency

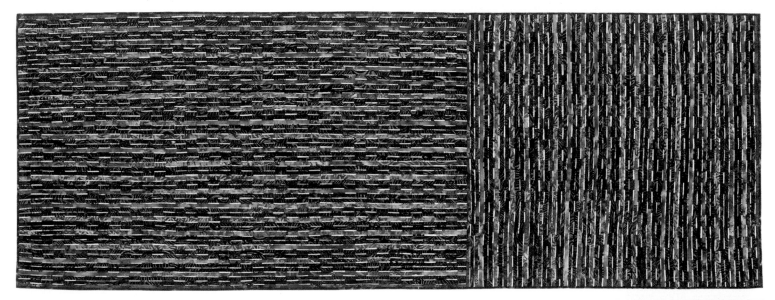

▲ Jarrahdale: Winter Tracks | 2005
21 x 56 feet (6.4 x 17 m)
Commercial cotton, cotton blend prints,
rayon, silk, ink; overdrawing,
machine stitched

Photos by Acorn Photo Agency

" I enjoy exploring subtle patterns that can go unnoticed—

patterns in life, the landscape, the built environment—

and expressing them through line and color. **"**

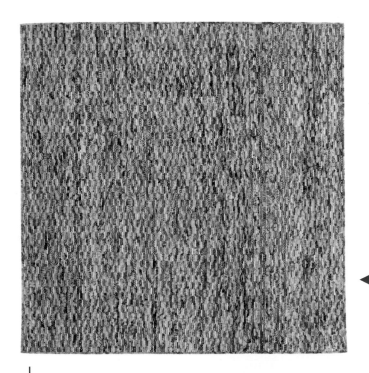

◀ Waiting for the Rain | 2004
48 x 48 inches (122 x 122 cm)
Cottons, cotton blends, lamé blend, rayon;
monoprinted, machine stitched

Photo by Acorn Photo Agency

▲ Indian Summer | 2006

29½ x 29½ inches (75 x 75 cm)
Commercial cottons, cotton blends,
rayon, textile ink; overdrawing,
machine stitched

Photo by Acorn Photo Agency

" Using fabric
scraps triggers
personal memories.
Reworking these
fabrics grounds me
in what has gone
before and is, for
me, a remaking
of the past. It's a
process that helps
me make sense of
the world. "

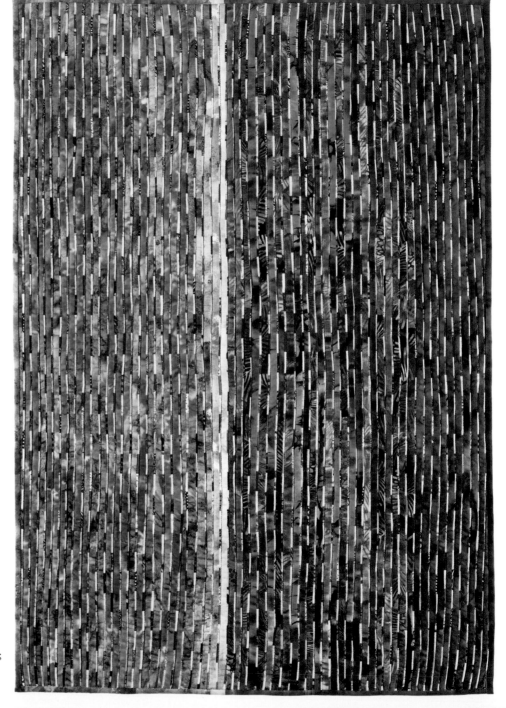

Iceline (Weave #4) | 2003 ▶
36³/₁₆ x 25³/₁₆ inches (92 x 64 cm)
Commercial cotton, cotton blend,
lamé blend, rayon, silk, textile ink;
overdrawing, machine stitched
Photo by Acorn Photo Agency

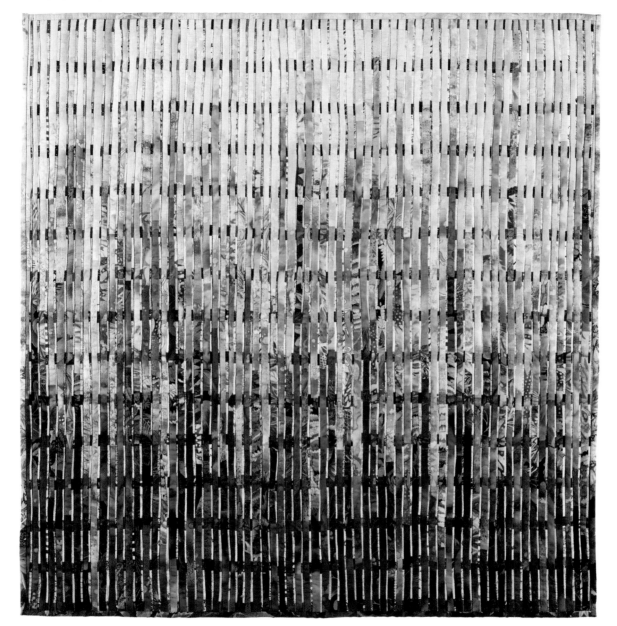

▲ Garden #2: Liquid Amber | 2004

27⁹⁄₁₆ x 27⁹⁄₁₆ inches (70 x 70 cm)
Cotton, cotton blends, rayon, textile ink;
overdrawing, machine stitched

Photo by Acorn Photo Agency

Linda MacDonald

HUMOR IS A TIME-HONORED VEHICLE for conveying sensitive messages, and quilts have long been used to promote political points of view. Quilts like those by Linda MacDonald communicate serious content in ways that make people smile.

MacDonald is concerned about the environmental problems that plague northern California, including logging, oil pumping, and overpopulation. To make her amusing, issue-oriented pieces, she creates whole cloth painted surfaces, which she hand quilts to add texture and emphasis. MacDonald paints primarily with an airbrush. For each quilt, she creates a full-size pattern on freezer paper, which she cuts out and irons onto her fabric. She then removes sections of the pattern and airbrushes them individually. Final details are hand painted before quilting.

MacDonald's bold, graphic images bring to mind comic-book art. The outlines are made of strong black lines highlighted with white, while the colors are unnatural or hyper-realistic. Many of the vignettes featured in her quilts are vaguely ominous. Some scenes rely on unexpected juxtapositions—trees and laptops, or animated oil pumps.

Whatever their content, her compelling fantasies always contain important truths for the viewer to contemplate.

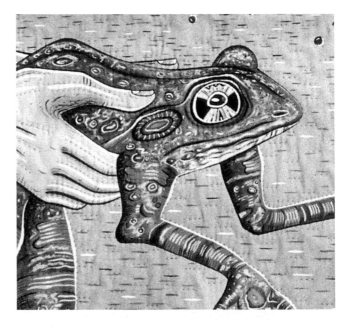

▲ **Migration of the California Red-Legged Frog** | 2002

39 x 36 inches (99.1 x 91.4 cm)

Cotton, acrylic paint, thread; airbrushed, stitched

Photos by Hap Sakwa

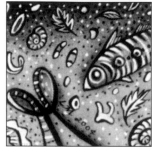

◀ **Child Labor** | 2004

20 x 20 inches (50.8 x 50.8 cm)
Cotton, acrylic paint, thread;
airbrushed, stitched

Photos by Bob Comings

Freedom | 2004 ▶

20 x 20 inches (50.8 x 50.8 cm)
Cotton, acrylic paint, thread;
airbrushed, stitched

Photos by Bob Comings

▲ **Spotted Owl vs. Chainsaw: Trespasser** | 1992

65 x 51 inches (1.6 x 1.3 m)

Cotton, acrylic paint, fiber-reactive dyes, thread; airbrushed, stitched

Photo by Amy Melious

▲ Town News | 1997

30 x 40 inches (76.2 x 101.6 cm)
Cotton, acrylic paint, fiber-reactive dyes, thread;
airbrushed, stitched

Photo by Amy Melious

" I use the design elements of pattern, symmetry, and static

imagery to create levels of interest and intrigue in my work.

I love being inventive with patterns. "

LINDA MACDONALD

▲ **Mountain Lion in the City** | 2006

20 x 20 inches (50.8 x 50.8 cm)
Cotton, acrylic paint, thread; airbrushed, stitched
Photo by Bob Comings

▲ **Even the Old Growth Must Work for Its Keep** | 2002

47 x 32 inches (119.4 x 81.3 cm)

Cotton, acrylic paint, thread; airbrushed, stitched

Photo by Hap Sakwa

▲ **Wildlife Sanctuaries** | 2002

36 x 45 inches (91.4 x 114 cm)
Cotton, acrylic paint, thread; airbrushed, stitched
Photo by artist

" I like working with basic cartoon images and flat color areas. I use these elements
when I want to portray a serious issue, in order to simplify my presentation. The effect
I'm going for is that of a story presented as a fantasy, with truthful ideas added. "

LINDA MACDONALD

▲ **Drive-Thru Trees** | 2001

28 x 44 inches (71.1 x 111.8 cm)
Cotton, acrylic paint, thread;
airbrushed, stitched

Photo by Hap Sakwa

" Images and ideas come first.

Techniques bring them to life. "

▲ **Love in the Forest** | 2006
   20 x 20 inches (50.8 x 50.8 cm)
   Cotton, acrylic paint, thread; airbrushed, stitched
   Photo by Bob Comings

Fenella Davies

THE FLEETING IMAGE OF A WATER DROPLET on an aged Venetian wall possesses the sort of forceful contrast that Fenella Davies finds infinitely inspiring. She savors visual interplay. To convey the beauty of worn, crumbling walls in Venice, Italy, or in Bath, England, where she lives, Davies collages torn pieces of loosely woven fabric, as well as strips of pleated, lightweight lead flashing, using them to punctuate the heavily painted, dyed, and rusted fibers of her backgrounds. Small highlights of bright red, turquoise, or golden yellow convey the play of light against the varied textures of ancient buildings.

Davies searches flea markets and antique stores for old, damaged fabrics, as their visible history of use conveys the passage of time. She avoids obvious quilting lines. To quilt her pieces, she employs a large darning needle and a long backstitch, which is done from the reverse of the piece. Davies uses couched thread circles to represent significant images—the sun in its movement, or the halos created by water bubbles. Contrasts of shape, color, form, and material create dynamic juxtapositions in her work, communicating at once a sense of life's transitory nature and time's slow, inexorable decay.

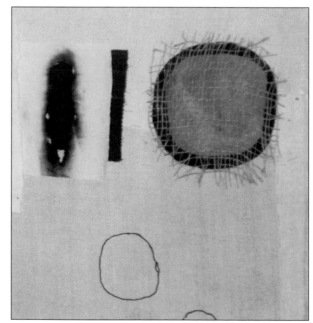

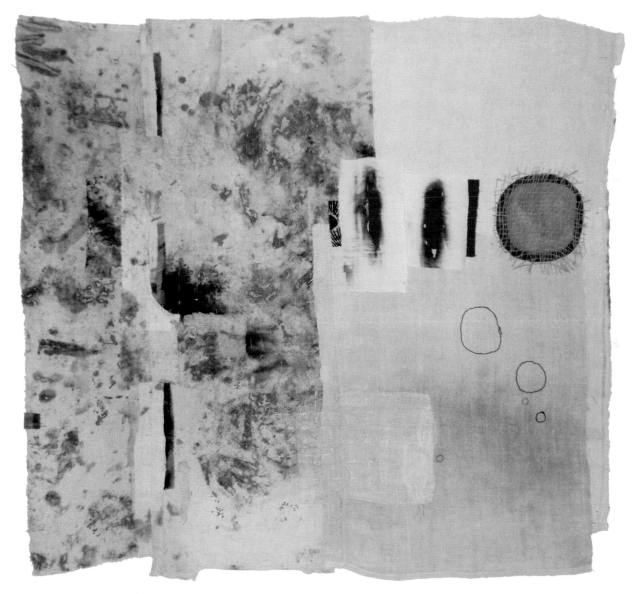

▲ Venetian Fire | 2009
   39³⁄₈ x 40³⁄₁₆ inches (100 x 102 cm)
   Antique linen smock, hessian, cotton;
   rusted, dyed, burned, hand sewn
   Photos by F. Martin

fenella Davies 2007

▲ **Venice: All Patched Up** | 2008

28 x 33 inches (71.1 x 13 cm)
Antique cottons and linens; hand dyed, painted,
bleached, hand sewn, machine sewn

Photo by F. Martin

" I try to play up the unique qualities of fabric—rough
linen, torn edges, and visible stitches. I love using
my medium to its fullest. **"**

DAVIES

FENELLA

▲ Venetian Reflections | 2008

40³⁄₁₆ x 43⁵⁄₁₆ inches (102 x 110 cm)

Antique cottons and linens, scrim; rusted, painted, dyed, reverse appliquéd

Photo by F. Martin

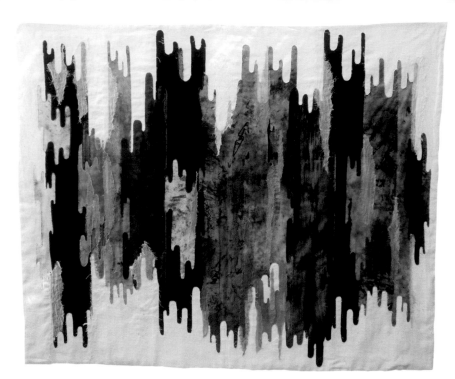

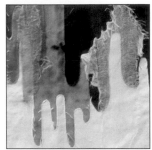

◄ **Australian Bushfires** | 2009

46¹⁄₁₆ x 57⁷⁄₈ inches (1.1 x 1.4 m)
Antique cotton and linen, scrim;
bleached, rusted, reverse appliquéd,
hand sewn

Photos by F. Martin

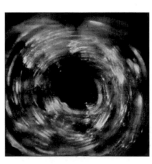

Winter Sun-Venezia | 2005 ►

59¹⁄₁₆ x 59¹⁄₁₆ inches (1.5 x 1.5 m)
Linen, cotton; painted, bleached,
hand sewn

Photos by F. Martin

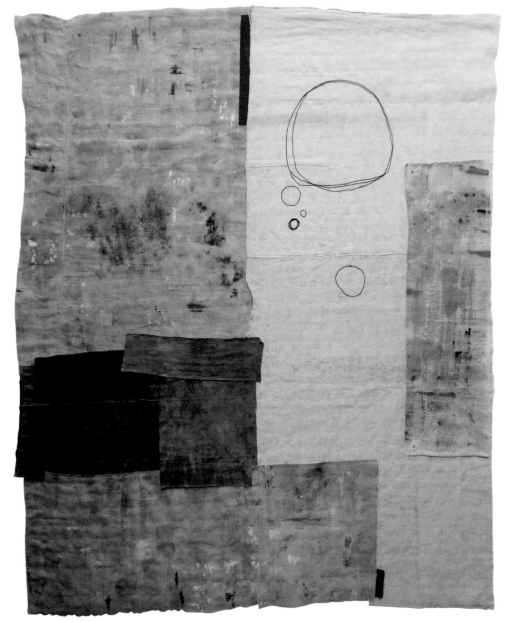

" I studied embroidery
and quilting to
master the technical
skills involved. Then
I rejected nearly
everything I learned
in order to free
myself creatively. "

▲ Reflections on a Venetian Wall | 2006
57⅛ x 46⅞ inches (1.4 x 1.2 m)
Antique French linens; hand dyed, rusted,
machine collaged, hand sewn
Photos by F. Martin

FENELLA DAVIES

▲ Venetian Flotsam | 2007

61 x 61 inches (1.5 x 1.5 m)
Antique linen, found cottons, scrim; hand painted
and dyed, hand sewn, machine sewn

Photo by F. Martin

▲ Venice: Windswept Papers | 2008

39⅜ x 39⅜ inches (100 x 100 cm)
Antique linen, scrim, found fabric; bleached,
painted, machine sewn, hand sewn
Photo by F. Martin

FENELLA **DAVIES**

DAVIES

FENELLA

▲ **Linear Movement 4** | 2000

53 x 64 inches (1.3 x 1.6 m)
Cotton; hand dyed, stitched, reverse appliquéd,
machine quilted, hand quilted

Photo by F. Martin

" Bold geometric designs and abstract compositions

provide the basis for my collaged cloth pieces. "

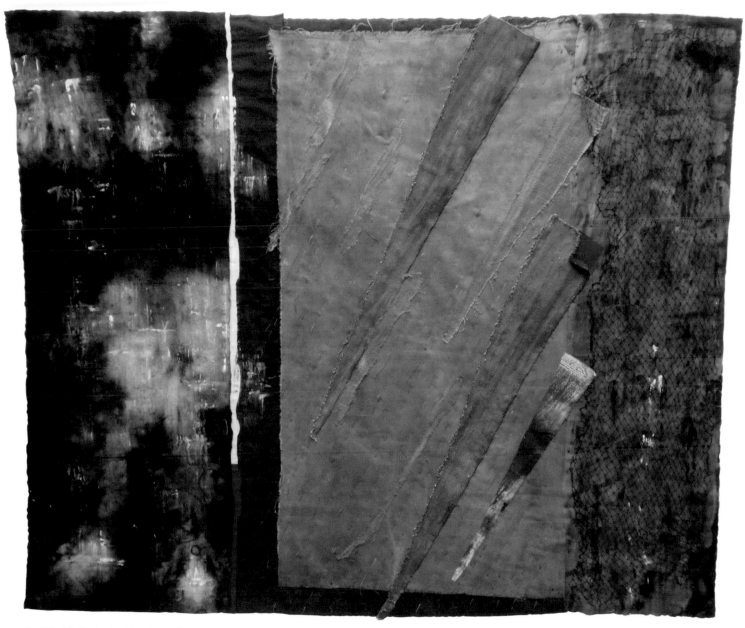

▲ Night Rain in Venice | 2009
$41\frac{3}{8}$ x $50\frac{3}{8}$ inches (1 x 1.3 m)
Antique linen, antique netting, hessian, mudcloth;
hand painted, hand sewn, machine sewn

Photo by F. Martin

Rachel Brumer

DAILY ROUTINES AND RITUALS mark the passage of time in our lives. Rachel Brumer explores this idea and our memorialization of loved ones in her evocative work through the use and repetition of symbolic images. She collects many of these motifs—birds, grave markers, and flower wreaths—during visits to local cemeteries. Other images, such as beds and dresses, come from daily life. Brumer photographs these items and then uses a Van Dyke Brown printing technique to transfer the negatives onto hand-dyed cloth. To create the exact look she wants, she may also use inks, silk-screen, text, or French knots.

A former modern dancer, Brumer is used to communicating ideas through pattern and repetition. In the dance studio, counting was used to mark the passage of time in a piece, and it now figures prominently in her work. The tracking of time is a theme Brumer returns to again and again. Hatch marks, images of bread loaves that symbolize our daily bread, and boot soles that bring to mind our journey through the day often appear in her complex textile constructions. By inviting viewers to interpret the meaning of her images, Brumer asks that we take the time to reflect upon our own significant symbols and the memories they conjure.

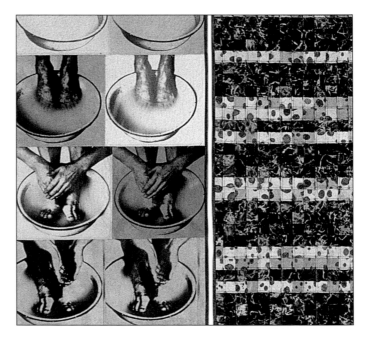

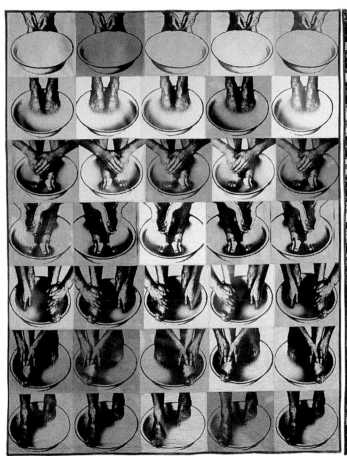 

▲ **Describing Rain** | 2004

84 x 120 inches (2.1 x 3 m)
Cotton; hand dyed, Van Dyke printed,
painted, machine pieced, hand quilted

Photos by Mark Frey

▲ Triplets | 1995

55 x 55 inches (1.4 x 1.4 m)
Cotton; hand dyed, Van Dyke printed, drawn, stitched,
stamped, hand appliquéd, machine pieced, hand quilted

Photo by Mark Frey

Coral Pollen Pearls | 2003 ▶

60 x 60 inches (1.5 x 1.5 m)
Cotton, silk dupioni; hand dyed,
screen-printed, French knotted,
hand appliquéd, hand quilted

Photos by Mark Frey

◀ Fanny Sosnowik 2/11/31 | 1997

67 x 66 inches (1.7 x 1.6 m)
Cotton, dye sticks; hand dyed, Van Dyke printed,
hand appliquéd, machine pieced, hand quilted

Photos by Mark Frey

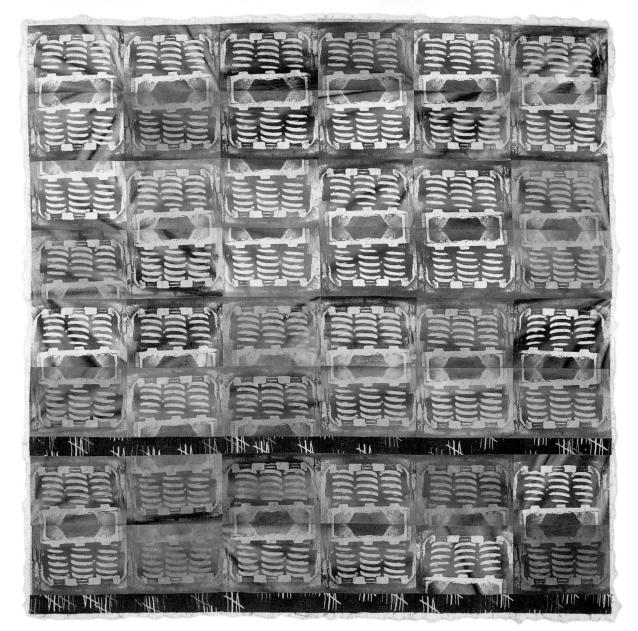

▲ Sarah Kurc 2/11/28 | 1997

68 x 70 inches (1.7 x 1.8 m)
Cotton; hand dyed, Van Dyke printed, silk-screened,
machine pieced, hand quilted

Photo by Mark Frey

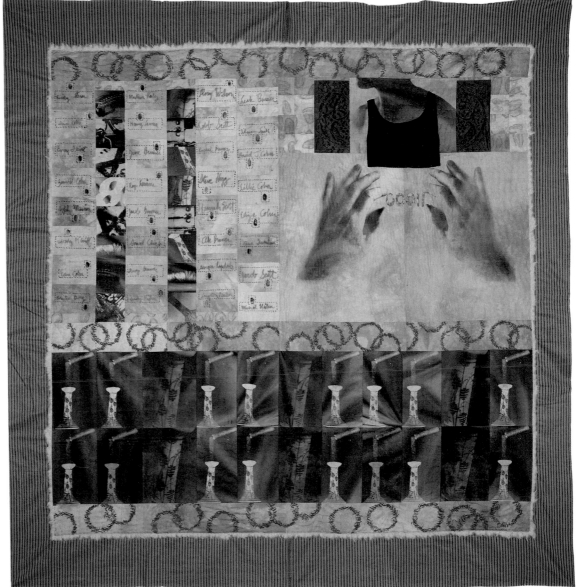

" My quilts
are visual
representations
of my ideas
about life. "

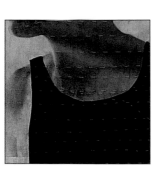

▲ Paula Jonap 2/11/25 | 1997

81 x 94 inches (2 x 2.4 m)
Cotton, dye stick; hand dyed, Van Dyke printed, silk-screened,
hand appliquéd, machine pieced, hand quilted
Photos by Mark Frey

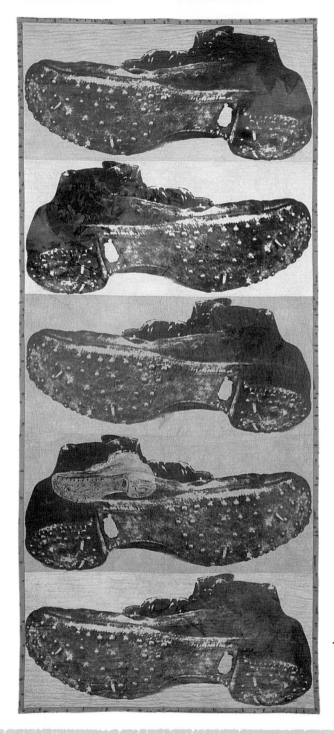

" Although my quilts are far from traditional, they're still connected to the history of the medium. The creation of beauty and meaning from a piece of fabric, the repetition of imagery, and the development of patterns all tie my work to tradition. "

◄ Fay Fuller's Boot | 1998

104 x 46 inches (2.6 x 1.2 m)
Cotton, silk dupioni; hand dyed, Van Dyke printed, machine pieced, hand quilted
Photo by Mark Frey

▲ Françoise Kadosh 2/11/26 | 1997

70 x 70 inches (1.8 x 1.8 m)
Cotton, dye sticks; hand dyed, Van Dyke printed, silk-screened,
hand appliquéd, machine pieced, hand quilted

Photo by Mark Frey

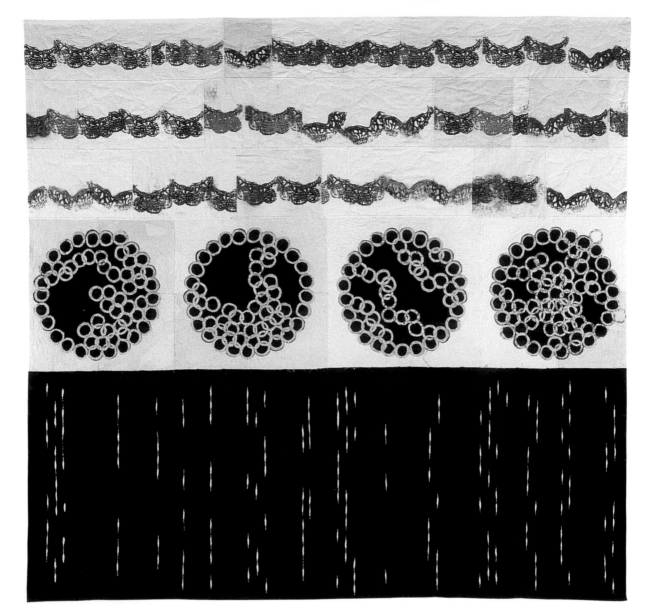

▲ Least Lightness | 2006

68 x 70 inches (1.7 x 1.8 m)
Cotton, linen; hand dyed, screen-printed, appliquéd,
reverse appliquéd, French knotted, machine pieced,
hand quilted

Photo by Mark Frey

RACHEL BRUMER

" I have an
unflagging
commitment to
fiber. I'm a firm
believer in the
communicative,
expressive,
healing power of
the medium. "

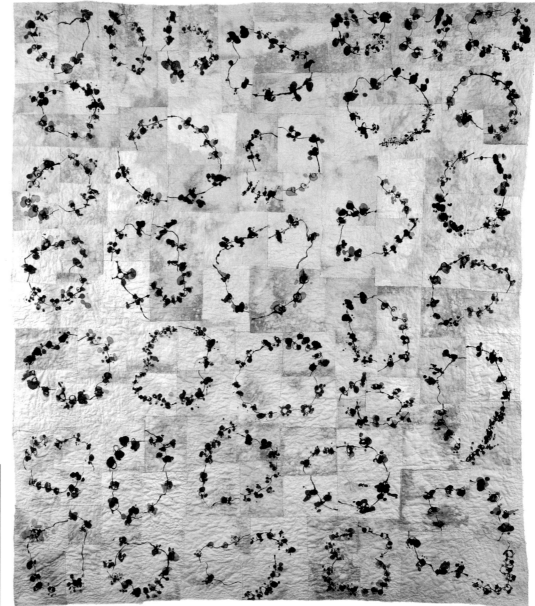

▲ Long Time Passing II | 2007
 72 x 62 inches (1.8 x 1.5 m)
 Cotton; hand dyed, discharged,
 painted, hand quilted
 Photos by Mark Frey

RACHEL **B**RUMER

Maryline Collioud-Robert

WHETHER SHE'S CREATING appliquéd mosaic structures or experimenting with novel variations of the pieced log-cabin block, Maryline Collioud-Robert uses her work to explore the ways in which colors interact to form intense textile surfaces. During her daily walks in Switzerland, when Collioud-Robert sees a combination of hues that she wants to capture, she writes down a list of related adjectives in a small notebook so she can recreate that combination of colors in fabric. Color is her main source of inspiration.

Collioud-Robert's work is often precisely cut and appliquéd. With a machine, she gives each individual shape a careful edging of blanket stitching in a different thread color. Other quilts feature raw-edge appliqué, with unraveling edges that create soft lines.

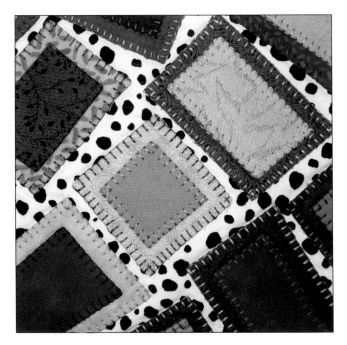

The repetition of shapes in her work reflects the flow of daily life with its repetitive tasks, while subtle variations in pieced backgrounds show how the world around us isn't always under our control. As Collioud-Robert obsessively arranges her jewel-like colors, she creates magical effects of light and dark—effects that make each encounter with her art unforgettable.

▲ **Stamps 2** | 2006

32¹¹⁄₁₆ x 41¾ inches (0.8 x 1 m)
Cotton; fused, machine appliquéd,
machine quilted

Photos by artist

" My mother was a seamstress at home when I was born. Fabrics and ribbons were my first toys. "

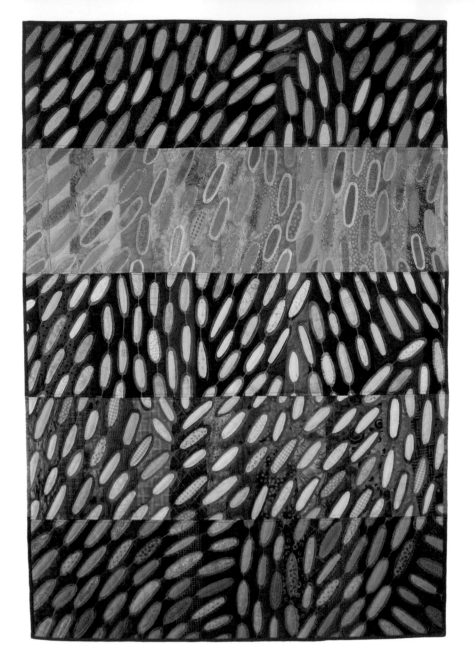

▲ Collage 3 | 2009
49³/₁₆ x 33⁷/₁₆ inches (1.2 x 0.8 m)
Cotton; fused, machine appliquéd, machine quilted
Photo by artist

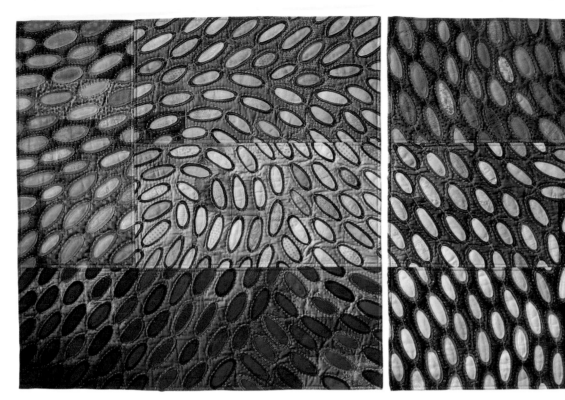

▲ Gujarat | 2008

33⅞ x 67⁹⁄₁₆ inches (0.8 x 1.7 m)
Cotton; fused, machine appliquéd,
machine quilted

Photo by artist

▼ Continuum | 2009

18⅞ x 87⅝ inches (0.4 x 2.2 m)
Cotton; machine pieced, machine quilted

Photo by artist

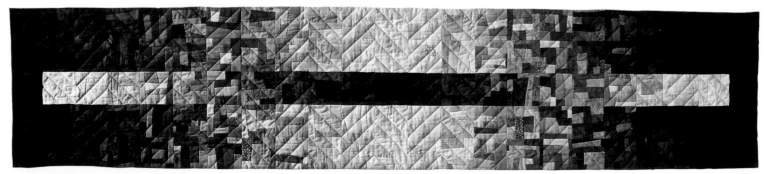

▲ White Is White | 2008

51³/₁₆ x 43⁵/₁₆ inches (1.3 x 1.1 m)

Cotton; machine pieced, machine appliquéd, hand quilted

Photo by artist

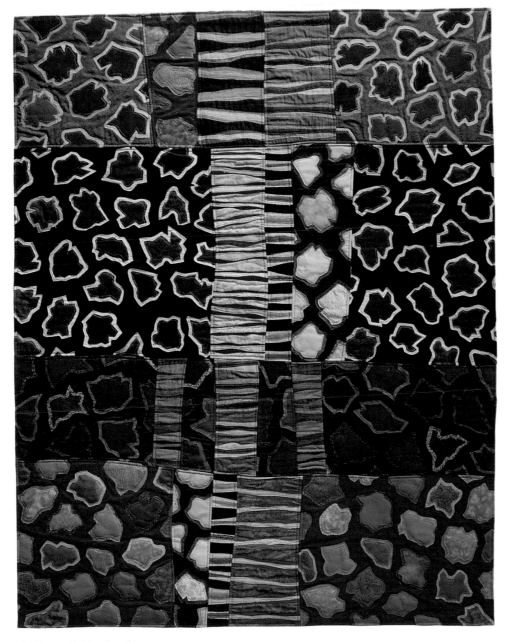

▲ Desert Study | 2002

53⅛ x 41¾ inches (1.3 x 1 m)

Cotton; fused, machine appliquéd, machine quilted

Photo by artist

" I like working with commercial fabrics. I like the idea of creating something personal using material that's available to everybody. "

Collage 1 | 2001 ▶
54¹¹⁄₁₆ x 35 inches (1.3 x 0.9 m)
Cotton; fused, machine appliquéd,
machine quilted
Photo by artist

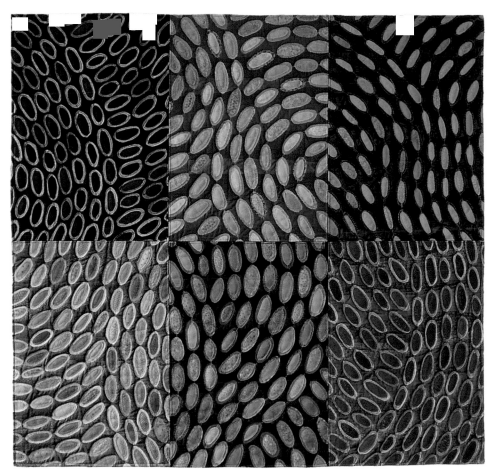

▲ **Collage 2** | 2006

38¹⁵⁄₁₆ x 41⁵⁄₁₆ inches (0.9 x 1 m)
Cotton; fused, machine appliquéd, machine quilted
Photo by artist

" I usually make collage works, but sometimes I feel the need to
piece hundreds of bits of fabric. I arrange, pin, and sew for weeks.
It's like meditation. "

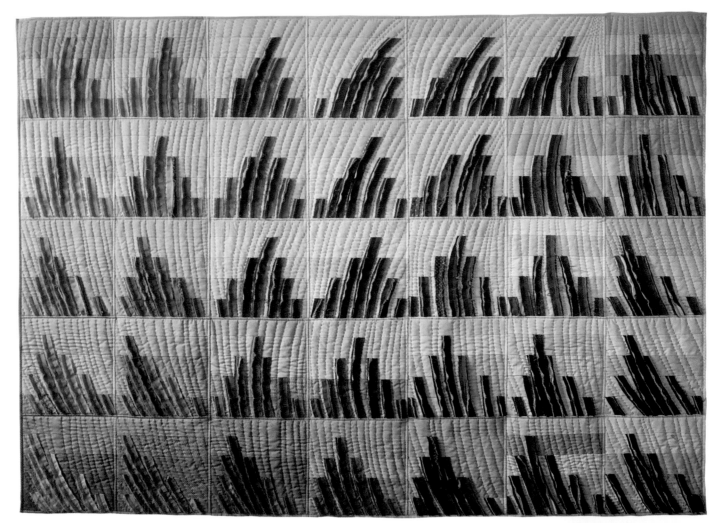

▲ **Quelques Herbes** | 1998

46^{7}/$_{16}$ x 64^{1}/$_{16}$ inches (1.2 x 1.6 m)

Cotton; machine pieced, hand quilted

Photos by artist

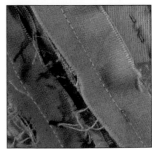

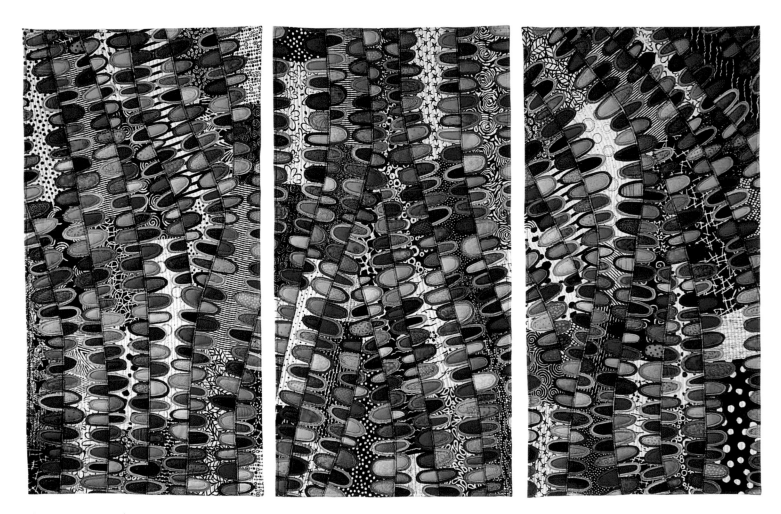

▲ Ciao Bella! | 2009

44¹/₁₆ x 67³/₁₆ inches (1.2 x 1.7 m)

Cotton; fused, machine appliquéd, machine quilted

Photo by artist

Jim Smoote

COMBINING POWERFUL PAINTED PORTRAITS with bold pieced designs, Jim Smoote creates quilts that are visually compelling. While his early work was inspired by jazz, African masks, and fetish figures, his recent pieces are riffs on contemporary pop culture and the hip-hop scene of Chicago, his hometown.

Using polyester interfacing as his canvas, Smoote paints dynamic figures in acrylics, then appliqués them by hand onto a pieced background. To set off the men and women depicted in his work, he creates dramatic graphic designs. He favors stripes, using them in his piecing or painting them with pearlized acrylic glaze. Sequins appear frequently as embellishments, while appliquéd symbols and signs offer clues to the inner thoughts of his subjects. Smoote machine quilts each work using metallic threads.

Exploring contemporary issues of gender and race, his work reflects an eclectic sensibility that draws from a wide-ranging visual library of 1970s funk art, African culture, and traditional Americana. Smoote skillfully synthesizes all of these elements and more in his irresistible quilts.

▲ **Sometimes I Can't Stand Myself!** | 2009

53 x 57 inches (1.3 x 1.4 m)
Cotton, satin, silk, acrylic paint, sequins;
machine pieced, hand appliquéd, hand quilted

Photos by artist

▲ Dwana | 2007

50 x 56 inches (1.2 x 1.4 m)
Cotton and assorted fabrics, acrylic paint,
sequins; machine pieced, hand quilted
Photo by artist

▲ Bubble Bath | 2007

42 x 60 inches (1 x 1.5 m)
Cotton, printed cotton, acrylic
paint, sequins; machine pieced,
hand appliquéd and quilted

Photo by artist

" My work often begins with a clipping from print media—a photo or a graphic design. If a photo is the inspiration, I'll develop a line drawing and trace it onto white cotton fabric. The finished piece is usually a mixture of piecing, appliqué, or embellishment. "

▲ Swirl | 2007

37 x 56½ inches (0.9 x 1.4 m)
Cotton and assorted fabrics, acrylic
paint; machine pieced, hand quilted

Photos by artist

▲ **Serenity** | 2007

42 x 65 inches (1 x 1.6 m)
Cotton, assorted fabrics,
acrylic paint, sequins;
machine pieced, hand
appliquéd, hand quilted

Photos by artist

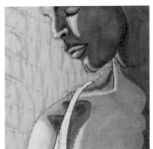

" I got my first taste of quilting during a summer vacation in Mississippi, when my mother took my siblings and me to a quilting bee. I was impressed with how the medium offered a sense of community while allowing the participants to express themselves individually. "

▲ Zen | 2008

47 x 47 inches (119.4 x 119.4 cm)
Cotton, polyester interfacing, assorted fabrics, acrylic paint;
machine pieced, hand appliquéd, hand quilted

Photo by artist

▲ Les Fleur Noir | 2009

49 x 46 inches (124.5 x 116.8 cm)
Cotton, assorted fabrics, polyester interfacing, acrylic paint;
machine pieced, hand appliquéd, hand quilted
Photo by artist

◀ **Diana Reeves** | 2005

43 x 46 inches
Cotton, polyester interfacing,
acrylic paint; hand appliquéd,
hand quilted

Photo by Robert Giesler

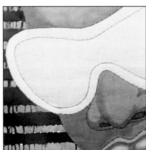

◀ **The Beef** | 2009

53 x 48 inches (1.3 x 1.2 m)
Cotton, commercial batik, assorted fabrics,
acrylic paint, sequins; machine pieced,
hand appliquéd, hand quilted

Photos by artist

▲ **Truth, Justice . . .** | 2009
 48 x 58 inches (1.2 x 1.4 m)
 Cotton, assorted fabrics, polyester interfacing,
 acrylic paint, sequins; machine pieced, hand
 appliquéd, hand quilted
 Photo by artist

" Quilting combines the best of what the art world has to give.

It can be sculptural. It can encompass drawing and painting.

It's the ultimate mixed medium. "

Eleanor McCain

DRAWN TO THE QUILT FORM because of family tradition—a grandmother and several other foremothers were quilters—Eleanor McCain values the ways in which the medium builds a sense of community. The quilt's potential for unlimited variation drives her to create in series—related works that explore color and spatial relationships. Her innovative quilts are experiments in pattern, contrast, and balance.

Basing her work on the simple nine-patch block, McCain takes that design to new heights. Always on the lookout for intriguing color combinations, she's inspired by the ways in which different hues play off each other. She machine pieces and quilts using an extensive palette of hand-dyed, solid fabrics.

Ranging from subtle to forceful, her colors make bold statements, intertwine gracefully, or fade quietly into the background. Block sizes expand and diminish. Lines follow a grid or wander randomly across a quilt's surface.

Always evocative and surprising, McCain's work brings to mind a wide-ranging variety of wonderful images—a mossy retreat, an urban skyscape, or a psychedelic 1970s party.

After Vale | 2008 ▶

85½ x 52½ inches (2.1 x 1.3 m)
Cotton; hand dyed, cut,
machine pieced,
machine quilted

Photos by Luke Jordan

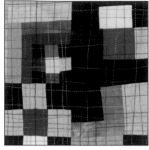

◀ **Nine-Patch Color Study 4** | 2007

    91 x 104 inches (2.3 x 2.6 m)
Cotton; hand dyed, cut,
machine pieced, machine quilted

    Photos by Luke Jordan

Alligators | 2008 ▶

84 x 108 inches (2.1 x 2.7 m)
Cotton; hand dyed,
cut, machine pieced,
machine quilted

Photos by Luke Jordan

ELEANOR **MCCAIN**

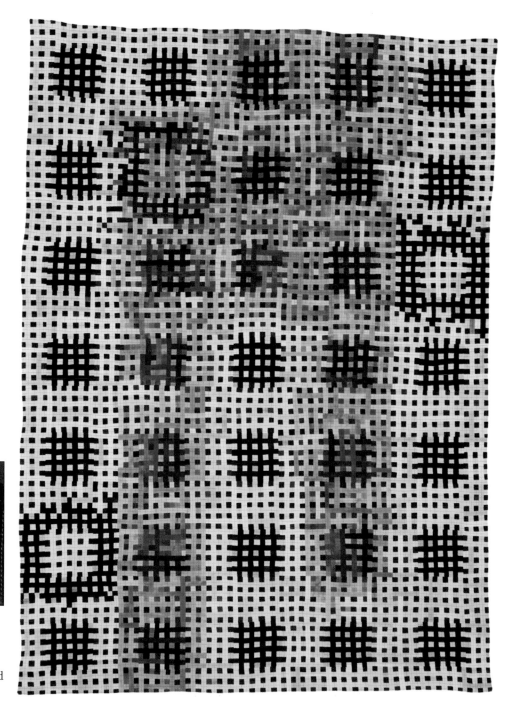

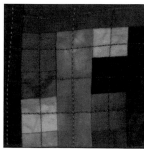

Moss 2 | 2006 ▶

98 x 70 inches (2.5 x 1.8 m)
Cotton; hand dyed, cut,
machine pieced, machine quilted
Photos by Luke Jordan

▲ Nine-Patch Color Study 5 | 2007

54 x 54 inches (1.3 x 1.3 m)
Cotton; hand dyed, cut, machine pieced, machine quilted

Photo by Luke Jordan

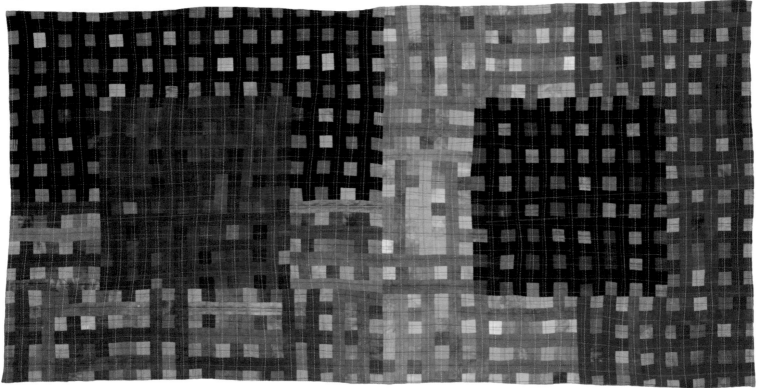

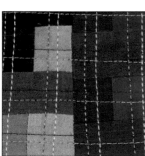

▲ **Six-Color Grid Study 1** | 2006

22 x 44 inches (55.9 x 111.8 cm)
Cotton; hand dyed, cut, machine pieced,
machine quilted

Photos by Luke Jordan

" I love working with fabric because of its sensuality,

its tactile intimacy, and its history. It has qualities

of texture, light absorption, and reflection that are

unmatched by any other medium. "

ELEANOR MCCAIN

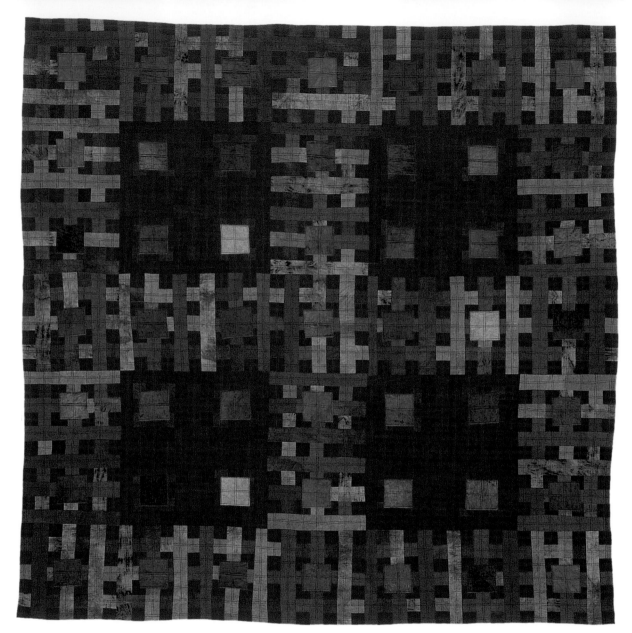

▲ Crab | 2002

90 x 90 inches (2.2 x 2.2 m)
Cotton; hand dyed, cut, machine pieced,
machine quilted

Photo by Luke Jordan

▲ **Crosses Study: Black and Yellow** | 2004

68 x 96 inches (1.7 x 2.4 m)
Cotton; hand dyed, cut, machine pieced,
machine quilted

Photo by Luke Jordan

" I feel connected to my ancestors and to other women who

have participated in this traditionally unrecognized art form.

It's important to me that my work has personal, historical,

and cultural relevance. **"**

▲ **Double Square Grid** | 2000

54 x 103 inches (1.3 x 2.6 m)
Cotton; hand dyed, cut, machine pieced,
machine quilted

Photos by Luke Jordan

" Quilting gives me a creative outlet that's grounded in family and
common experience. It also provides me with unlimited opportunities
for experimentation and aesthetic exploration. "

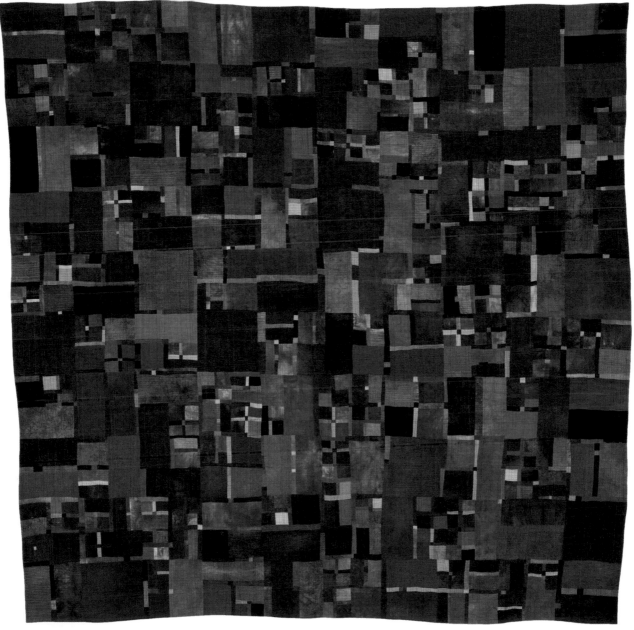

▲ **Green 2** | 2008

    104 x 104 inches (2.6 x 2.6 m)

    Cotton; hand dyed, cut, machine pieced, machine quilted

    Photo by Luke Jordan

ELEANOR MCCAIN

Patricia Malarcher

THE TENSION THAT EXISTS between the constraints of formal geometry and the freedom of improvisational collage runs through Patricia Malarcher's dynamic work. A New Jersey resident, Malarcher lives close to New York City's garment district, and that's where she discovered the vinyl-backed, metalized Mylar used in many of her quilts. The highly reflective Mylar showcases her machine-quilting lines, so that stitched patterns become a prominent component of each design. Thanks to the interplay between simple geometric pieced elements—especially checkerboards and stripes—and small jewel-like collages created from vintage textiles, found objects, and paint, Malarcher's work brings to mind ceremonial garments or elements from the world of architecture.

When her favorite Mylar fabrics became scarce, Malarcher began to experiment with other materials. She now creates her own surface designs through folding, blueprinting, and discharge. These recent pieces abandon the strict formality of her older work and are looser in their composition, with hand-stitched embellishments and random folds.

Complex in both material and construction, Malarcher's remarkable quilts offer a view into some alternate universe.

▲ Cloth of Honor | 2006

53 x 54 inches (1.3 x 1.3 m)
Mylar, canvas, brocade, paint, dye, thread, transfer prints;
screen-printed, hand sewn, machine sewn

Photos by D. James Dee

▲ **Alternating Currents** | 2003

48 x 48 inches (121.9 x 121.9 cm)
Fabric, Mylar, paint, leather, computer printing;
collaged, hand sewn, machine sewn

Photo by D. James Dee

" Sometimes I work with materials that I consider unattractive, like a set of fabric swatches in dull colors. I challenge myself to find ways of making these materials palatable—by applying gold leaf or overlays of screen-printing. "

◀ **Crossing** | 2000

52 x 30 inches (132.1 x 76.2 cm)
Fabric, Mylar, paint, gold leaf;
collaged, hand sewn,
machine sewn

Photos by D. James Dee

▲ **Climb** | 2002

    60 x 37 inches (1.5 x 0.9 m)
    Fabric, Mylar, paint, gold leaf,
    beads, digital prints; screen-printed,
    collaged, hand sewn, machine sewn
    Photo by D. James Dee

Tides | 2003 ▶

    52 x 18 inches (1.3 x 0.4 m)
    Fabric, Mylar, transfer print;
    discharged, blueprinted,
    hand sewn, machine sewn,
    appliquéd
    Photo by D. James Dee

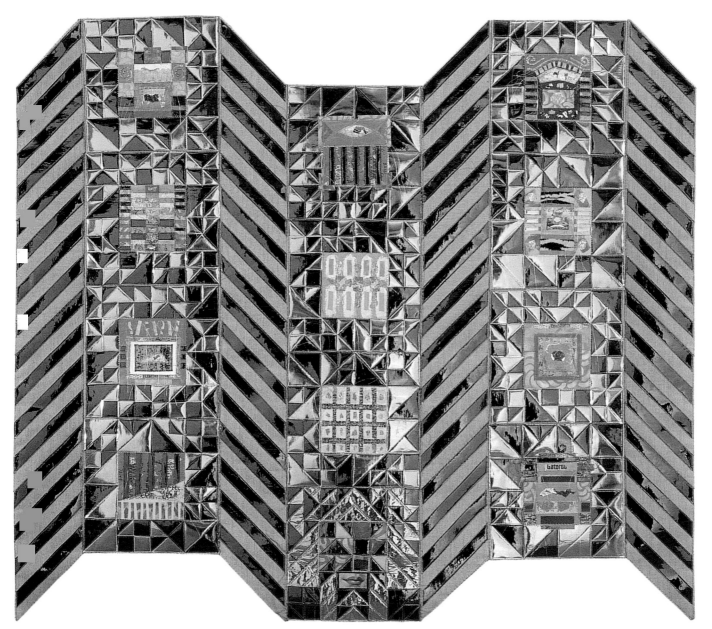

▲ Iconostasis | 1998

54 x 60 inches (1.3 x 1.5 m)
Fabric, Mylar, paint, mixed media;
collaged, hand sewn, machine sewn

Photo by D. James Dee

▲ January | 2005

13 x 18½ inches (33 x 47 cm)
Fabric, Mylar, transfer prints;
discharged, blueprinted, appliquéd,
hand sewn, machine sewn

Photo by D. James Dee

▲ **Solstice 1221** | 2005

13 x 18½ inches (33 x 47 cm)
Fabric, Mylar, transfer and Polaroid prints,
gold leaf; discharged, blueprinted,
machine sewn
Photo by D. James Dee

" My work combines a spectrum of ideas and materials.

Sewing allows for the co-existence of diverse elements. "

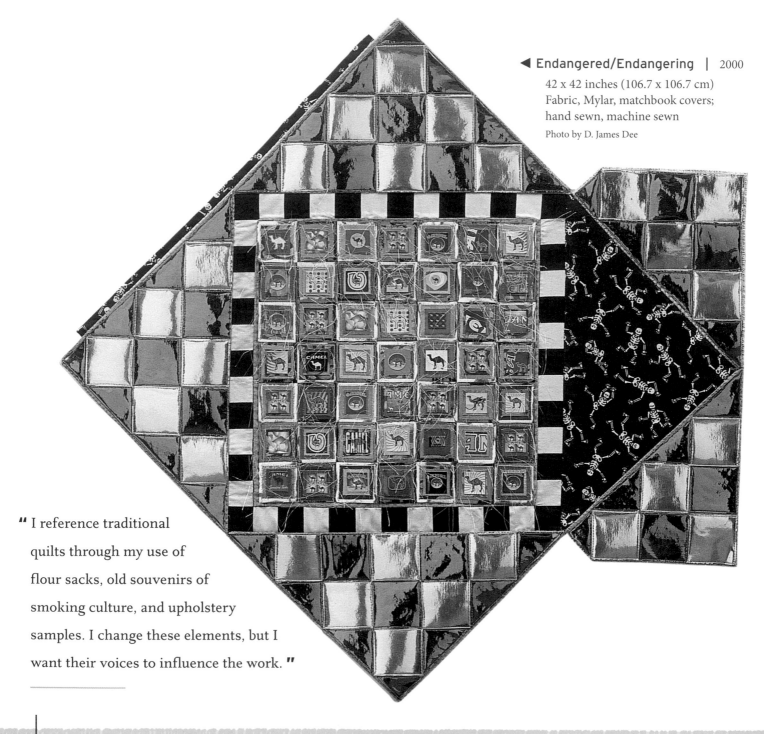

◀ **Endangered/Endangering** | 2000
42 x 42 inches (106.7 x 106.7 cm)
Fabric, Mylar, matchbook covers;
hand sewn, machine sewn
Photo by D. James Dee

" I reference traditional
quilts through my use of
flour sacks, old souvenirs of
smoking culture, and upholstery
samples. I change these elements, but I
want their voices to influence the work. "

▲ Game | 2003

48 x 42 inches (121.9 x 106.7 cm)
Fabric, Mylar, leather; collaged,
screen-printed, hand sewn,
machine sewn

Photo by D. James Dee

Misik Kim

MOST TRADITIONAL KOREAN *chogak po* patchwork is pieced in an orderly design, but some types resemble Western-style crazy quilts. Misik Kim's work builds on both of these traditions while taking them in decidedly new directions. Reflecting her love of nature and the serenity she finds in her daily routines, Kim's designs play with block sizes, shapes, and colors. Several pieces experiment with figure-ground relationships, as colors fade in and out of the background.

Kim hand dyes her own cottons, silks, satins, and linens in hues that reflect the changing seasons. To make the concentric squares and resist-dyed circles that flow across her surfaces, she uses piecing, appliqué, and reverse-appliqué. Each of her quilts is carefully balanced, yet the central focus is often slightly off-center.

Kim does her quilting and decorative stitching by hand and by machine, depending on the elements she wishes to accent. Her work is completely geometric, yet her choice of colors and block placement evokes different moods and images, ranging from the energy of leaves blown by the wind to the regret of fading memories. In Kim's work, as in traditional *chogak po*, many small pieces of fabric join together to become beautifully transformed.

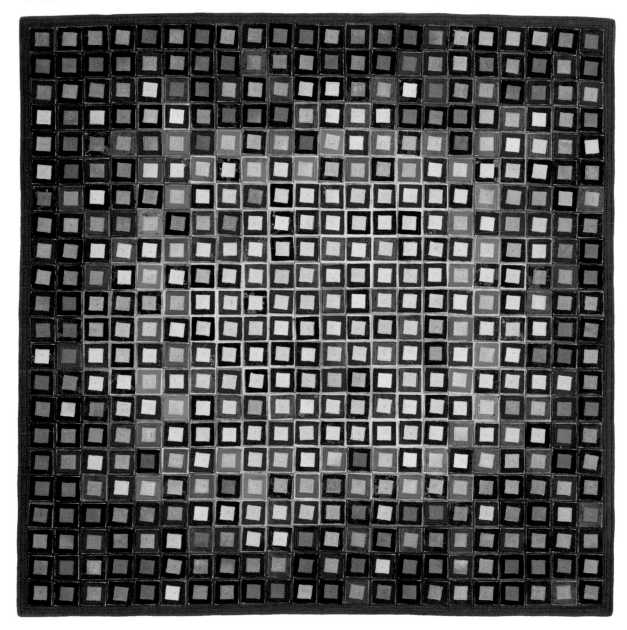

▲ The Play I | 2008
73¼ x 73¼ inches (1.8 x 1.8 m)
Cotton, silk; hand dyed, machine pieced,
machine quilted
Photos by Lee Man Hong

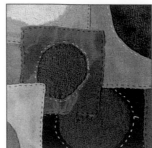

◀ **The Forest** | 2002

80¾ x 84¹¹⁄₁₆ inches (2 x 2.1 m)
Cotton; hand dyed, direct
appliquéd, reverse appliquéd,
hand quilted

Photos by Lee Man Hong

*" I like playing around with the sewing machine
and different fabrics. The experimentation frees
me from the fixed ideas that I unconsciously
follow when making quilts. "*

The Journey to the Past | 2005 ▶

74¹³⁄₁₆ x 70⁷⁄₈ inches (1.9 x 1.8 m)
Korean silk; machine pieced,
hand quilted

Photo by Lee Man Hong

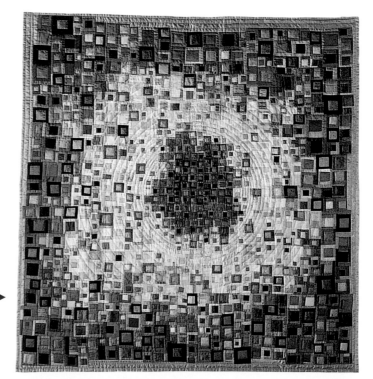

KIM
MISIK

▲ **One Day in the Spring** | 2003

$43^{5}/_{16}$ x $37^{7}/_{16}$ inches (110 x 95 cm)

Cotton; hand dyed, machine pieced, hand quilted

Photo by Lee Man Hong

" I think my
work is very
Korean. It has a
serenity that's
characteristic
of traditional
Korean culture. "

The Long Way | 2006 ▶
77³⁄₁₆ x 63 inches (1.9 x 1.6 m)
Cotton; hand dyed,
machine pieced, hand quilted
Photo by Lee Man Hong

▲ **The Wind** | 2005

66¹⁵/₁₆ x 70⅞ inches (1.7 x 1.8 m)

Cotton; hand dyed, machine pieced, hand quilted

Photo by Lee Man Hong

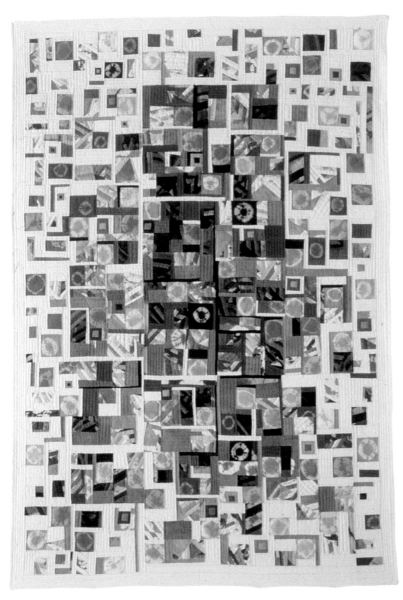

" I produce my
own colors by
hand dyeing
different fabrics.
By combining my
materials, I can
achieve a variety of
colors and shapes,
transforming them
into the images that
I want to create. "

◀ The Year Lost | 2002

72⅞ x 48¹³/₁₆ inches (1.8 x 1.2 m)
Cotton; hand dyed, machine pieced,
hand quilted
Photo by Lee Man Hong

▲ In the Mount Bookhan | 2005

66¹⁵⁄₁₆ x 65³⁄₈ inches (1.7 x 1.6 m)
Cotton; hand dyed, machine pieced, appliquéd, hand quilted

Photo by Lee Man Hong

▲ **The Road to the Forest** | 2002

50 x 50 inches (1.2 x 1.2 m)
Cotton; hand dyed, machine pieced, hand quilted
Photo by Lee Man Hong

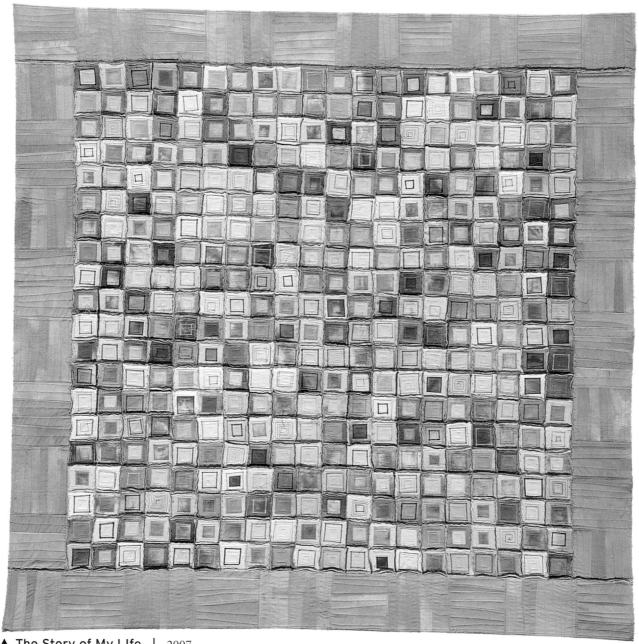

▲ **The Story of My LIfe** | 2007

52¾ x 52⅜ inches (1.3 x 1.3 m)

Cotton; hand dyed, machine pieced, hand quilted

Photo by Lee Man Hong

Elizabeth Busch

DREAMS AND VISIONS INTERSECT in Elizabeth Busch's provocative work. Unknown moons float across the sky. Bubbles of glowing color are partially concealed by curtains. Contrasting materials bring visual tension to her work, and spatial ambiguities keep viewers off balance. She creates her painted fabrics intuitively. Depending on her mood, she may use a carefully controlled airbrush or fling paint on a canvas and comb through it.

Busch tries not to have preconceptions about what her work will look like. She cuts and arranges painted fabrics, letting the colors and shapes lead her forward. Later reflection may reveal visual references to aspects of her life in Maine—a bridge against the night sky, creatures scuttling in rock pools—but each piece progresses without plans or drawings.

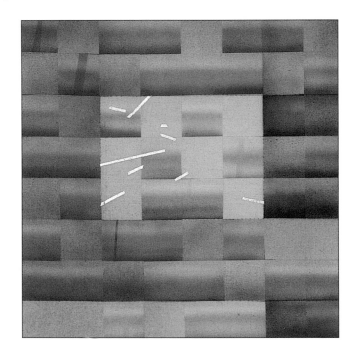

Hand quilting and embroidery bring the works down to a more human level, engaging Busch up close after the arm's-length process of creating the surface design. The translucency of glowing color contrasted with furrows of hand-quilted stitching draws the eye in for a closer look. The curtains pull aside, and viewers experience the full magic of Busch's cosmic tableaux.

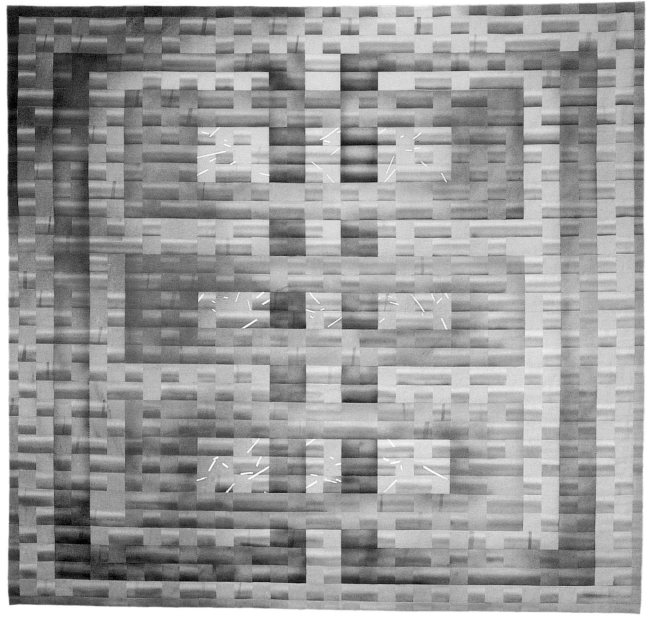

▲ Spring | 1998

66 x 69½ inches (1.6 x 1.7 m)
Cotton duck, whole cloth, acrylic paint, metal leaf;
hand painted, air brushed, hand quilted

Photos by Dennis Griggs

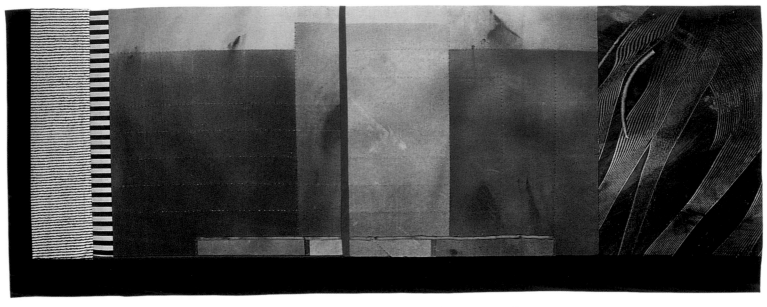

▲ Morning | 1995
16 x 42 inches (40.6 x 106.7 cm)
Cotton duck, cotton-polyester fabric, textile paint;
airbrushed, machine pieced, hand quilted, machine quilted
Photo by Dennis Griggs

" In the early 1980s I was making paintings on canvas, stretching them
on stretcher bars and framing them. The day I cut up a canvas changed
everything. In one fell swoop, paintings became art quilts. "

ELIZABETH BUSCH

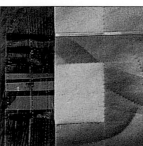

▲ **Transformation** | 1995

43 x 62 inches (1.1 x 1.5 m)
Cotton duck, cotton-polyester fabric,
textile paint; airbrushed, machine pieced,
hand quilted, machine quilted

Photos by Dennis Griggs

▲ Winter | 1998

67 x 69 inches (1.7 x 1.8 m)
Cotton duck, whole cloth, acrylic paint, metal leaf;
hand painted, airbrushed, hand quilted
Photo by Dennis Griggs

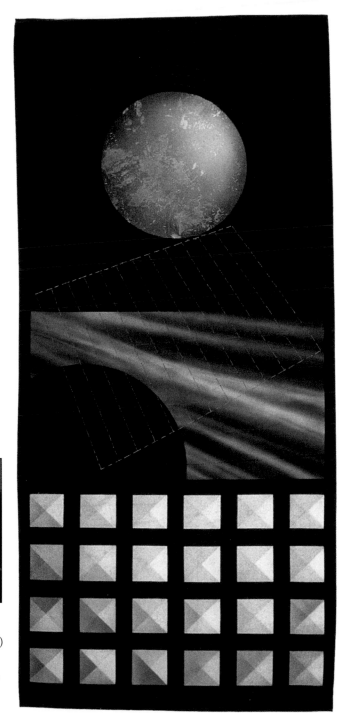

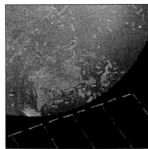

Return | 2005 ▶

39 x 18 inches (99.1 x 66 cm)
Cotton-polyester fabric;
airbrushed, machine pieced,
hand quilted

Photos by artist

▲ What It Was Like, What Happened, What It's Like Now | 2004

22 x 96 inches (0.6 x 2.4 m)
Cotton-polyester fabric; airbrushed,
machine pieced, hand quilted

Photo by artist

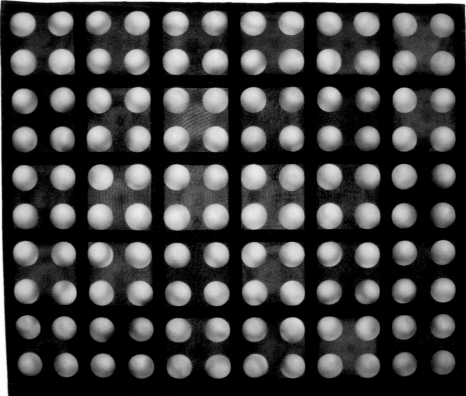

Echo | 2009 ▶

31½ x 37 inches (80 x 94 cm)
Cotton blend, whole cloth;
airbrushed, machine quilted,
hand quilted

Photos by artist

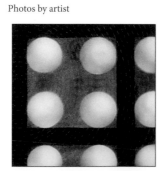

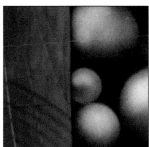

▲ Yellow | 2004

28½ x 74 inches (0.7 x 1.9 m)
Cotton duck, cotton-polyester fabric, textile paint;
airbrushed, machine pieced, hand quilted,
machine quilted

Photos by artist

" I hand quilt each piece. This part of the process allows me to become

physically acquainted with the quilt, to add an extra visual dimension to it. "

ELIZABETH BUSCH

▲ **Two Thousand Seven** | 2007

38 x 59 inches (0.9 x 1.5 m)
Cotton duck, cotton-polyester fabric;
painted, machine pieced, machine
quilted, hand quilted

Photo by artist

" I never know what I'm going to make until
it's actually happening. The head-heart
computer inside me lets me know it's time
for something to come out. "

▲ Imbalance | 2006

48 x 42 inches (121.9 x 106.7 cm)
Cotton duck, cotton-polyester fabric; painted,
machine pieced, machine quilted, hand quilted

Photo by artist

Dorothy Caldwell

INSPIRED BY THE FIELDS AND LAKES of eastern Ontario, Dorothy Caldwell creates enigmatic maps in cloth that provocatively explore mankind's relationship to the land. Many of Caldwell's quilts contain mysterious elliptical shapes that take on shifting identities, mutating into bowls, stones, or islands. Fascinated by the ways in which historical textiles reflect the passage of time through patching and mending, she tries to create a similar feeling in her work. She often scratches hundreds of tiny lines into her wax-resisted cloth to build up fields of stark black-and-white markings, which she punctuates with small appliquéd patches of brilliant color.

The physicality of creating her material is valued by Caldwell. She paints and prints with wax over black fabric, then scrapes and abrades the wax before discharging the uncovered parts to white. The cloth gains meaning as it's marked and stitched.

Caldwell's processes are slow. The laborious addition of elements over a period of time allows each of her pieces to gather meaning. They begin to reflect our primordial connection with the land.

▲ Two Lakes Joined | 2008

55 x 55 inches (1.4 x 1.4 m)
Cotton; wax resist, discharged, stitched,
appliquéd, silk-screened

Photos by Gary Mulcahey

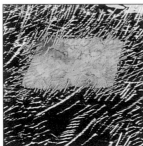

▲ **A Hill/A Lake** | 2002

18¹⁵⁄₁₆ x 59¹⁄₁₆ inches (0.4 x 1.5 m)
Cotton; wax resist, discharged,
stitched, appliquéd

Photos by Thomas Moore

▼ **An Island/A Pond** | 2002

18¹⁵⁄₁₆ x 59¹⁄₁₆ inches (0.4 x 1.5 m)
Cotton; wax resist, discharged,
stitched, appliquéd

Photos by Thomas Moore

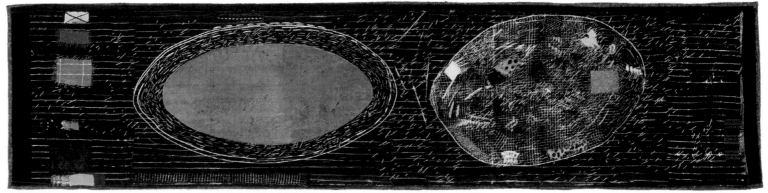

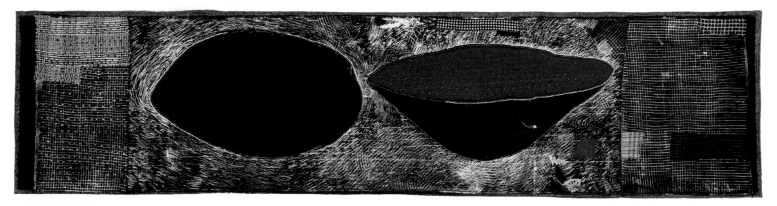

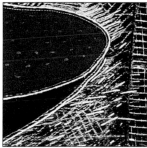

▲ A Lake/A Bowl | 2002

18¹⁵⁄₁₆ x 59¹⁄₁₆ inches (0.4 x 1.5 m)

Cotton; wax resist, discharged, stitched, appliquéd

Photos by Thomas Moore

" I have a deep respect for cloth. It's very powerful when it retains traces

of its previous life, gathers history, and becomes something new. "

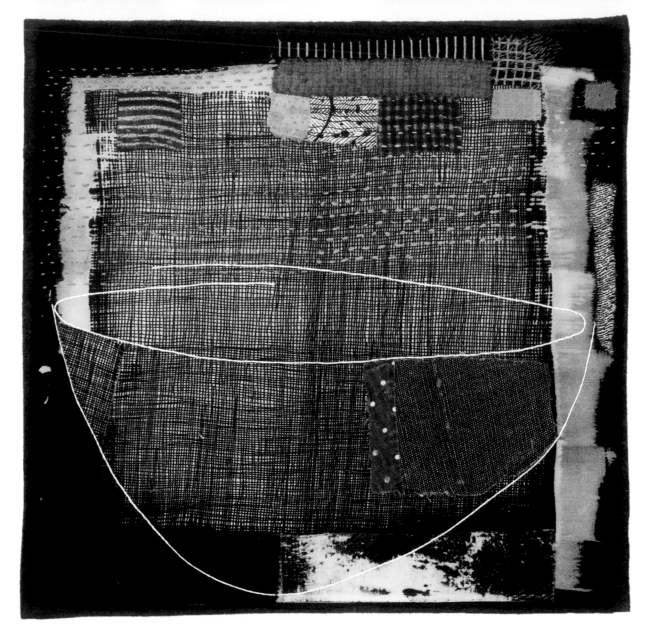

▲ Bowl | 2008

18⅛ x 18⅛ inches (46 x 46 cm)
Cotton; wax resist, discharged, silk-screened,
stitched, appliquéd

Photo by Trent Photography

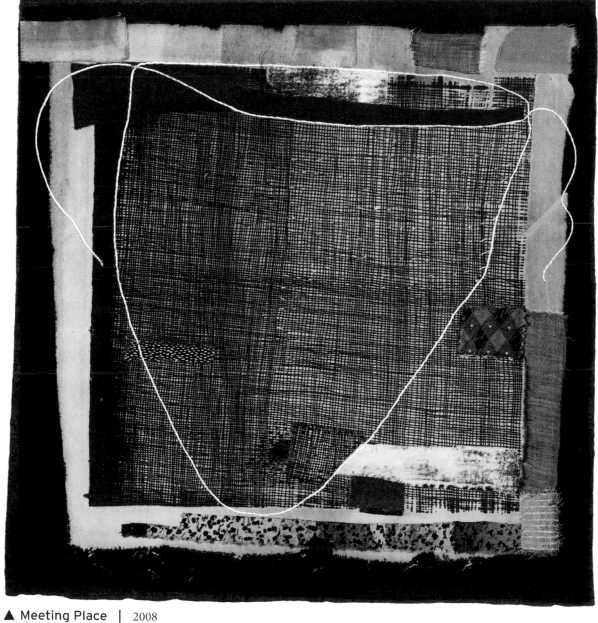

▲ Meeting Place | 2008

18⅛ x 18⅛ inches (46 x 46 cm)
Cotton; wax resist, discharged, silk-screened,
stitched, appliquéd
Photo by Trent Photography

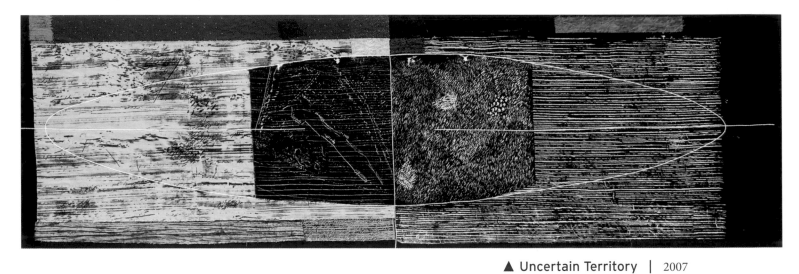

" Stitches accumulate like a journal of energy and experience. "

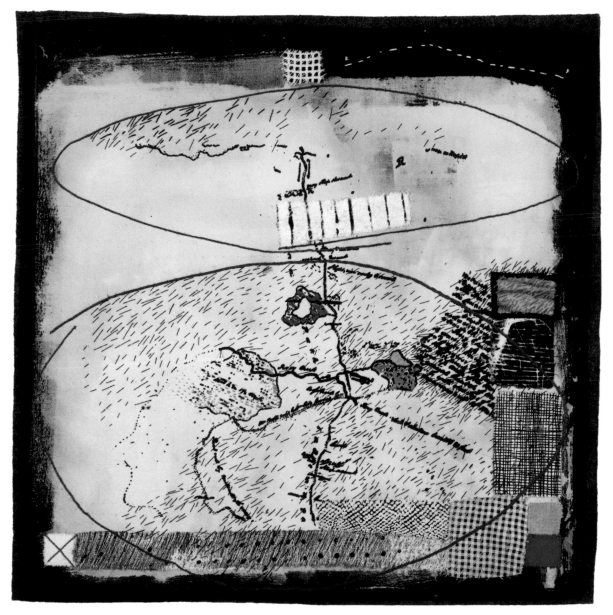

▲ Joined Lakes | 2008

18⅛ x 18⅛ inches (46 x 46 cm)
Cotton; wax resist, discharged, silk-screened,
stitched, appliquéd
Photo by Trent Photography

▲ Deep Lake/High Hill | 2007
21 x 74 inches (0.5 x 1.8 m)
Cotton; wax resist, discharged,
block printed, stitched, appliquéd
Photos by MAFU

" My work begins with a series of
calligraphic marks made using hot
wax as a resist. I'm energetic with
the cloth—I'm not afraid to gouge
into the wax. I court the accidental
and welcome the surprises that
happen during this process. **"**

▲ This Place | 2008

18⅛ x 18⅛ inches (46 x 46 cm)
Cotton; wax resist, discharged,
stitched, appliquéd

Photo by Trent Photography

DOROTHY CALDWELL

Tim Harding

IT'S NO ACCIDENT THAT SILK is the fabric used most frequently by Tim Harding. The material's reflective qualities make it the perfect choice for depicting water—a recurring subject in his work. To make his richly hued, lustrous quilts, Harding layers silk in several different shades and then cuts through the top layers to reveal the colors below. The patterns of his cut lines vary and can be grid-like, linear, straight, or wavy. Harding then folds, twists, or crushes the top layers of silk so that varying amounts of the colors underneath are revealed.

He chooses colors that either blend subtly together or vibrate against one another. The multiple layers allow for complex color interactions. His work has an illusion of depth and movement, as the upper layers alternately obscure and reveal images beneath the surface.

Harding is an avid experimenter when it comes to the interplay between form and image. For his Artifacts series, he created luminous, three-dimensional works using an origami-like folding process. Other pieces are two-sided and semi-transparent and feature shifting perspectives. In all of his work, Harding strives to express the moments of fleeting beauty he sees in the natural world.

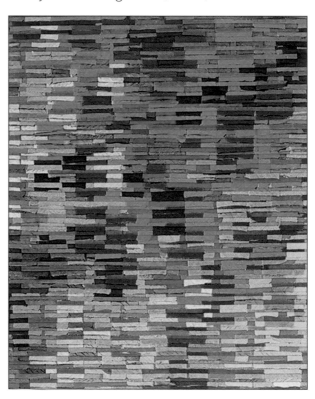

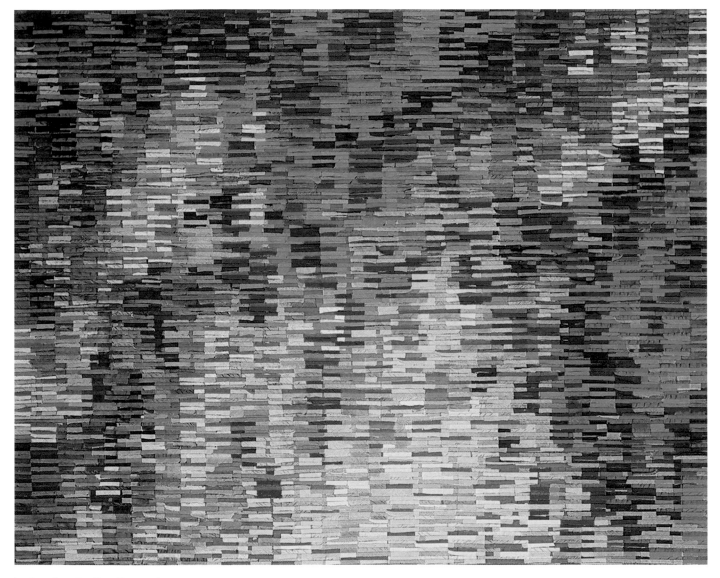

▲ Garden Reflections | 2008

53 x 67 inches (1.3 x 1.7 m)

Silk, cotton; collage layered, stitched, cut

Photos by P. Meyer/C. Hooker

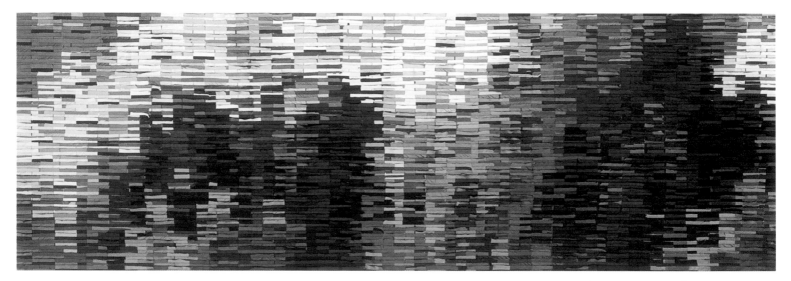

▲ Reflections | 2003
32 x 92 inches (81.3 x 233.7 cm)
Silk; collage layered, stitched, cut
Photo by P. Meyer/C. Hooker

" There's a culturally ingrained preciousness to fabric.

We mustn't tear, scorch, or soil our 'good' clothes.

My work is technically and conceptually based on the

act of violating this taboo. **"**

TIM HARDING

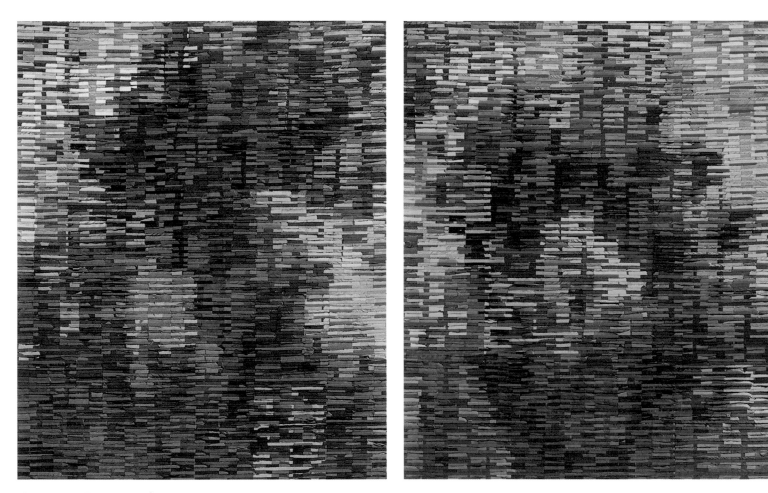

▲ Lake Reflections | 2006

58½ x 96 inches (1.4 x 2.4 m)
Silk, cotton; collage layered, stitched, cut

Photo by Petronella Ytsma

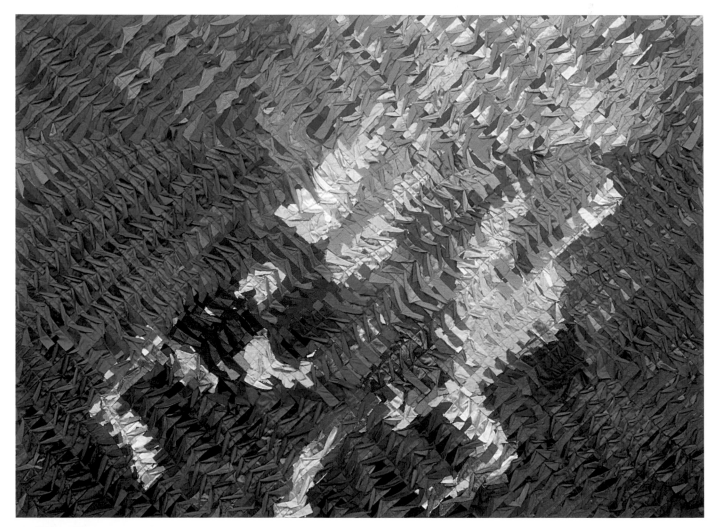

▲ **Swimmers** | 1998

60 x 80 inches (1.5 x 2 m)
Silk; collage layered, stitched, cut

Photos by Petronella Ytsma

▲ **Swimmer #4** | 1999

40 x 59 inches (1 x 1.5 m)
Silk; collage layered, stitched, cut

Photo by Petronella Ytsma

▲ Campo de Oro | 1999

60 x 96 inches (1.5 x 2.4 m)
Silk; collage layered, stitched, cut
Photo by Petronella Ytsma

" I'm intrigued by textiles and the wonderful qualities they possess—the tactile richness, the pliable plane, the inherent grid of the weave. "

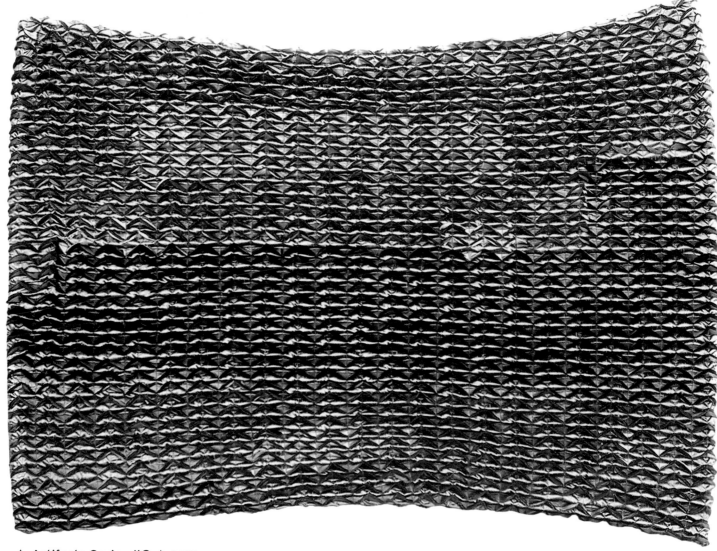

▲ **Artifacts Series #9** | 2007

34 x 45 inches (86.4 x 114.3 cm)

Silk, cotton; reverse appliquéd, collapse quilted

Photo by P. Meyer

▲ Koi #12 | 2000
37 x 48 inches (94 x 121.9 cm)
Silk; collage layered, stitched, cut
Photo by P. Meyer/C. Hooker

" I believe quilts spark subconsciously intimate connections in viewers, and this is what I strive for with my work. It's a way of diminishing the gap between art and life. "

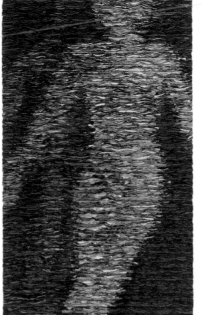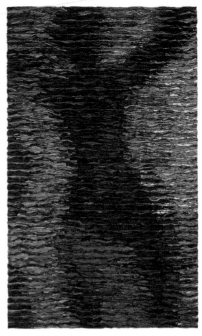

▲ Figures Triptych | 2005
    48 x 92 inches (1.2 x 2.3 cm)
    Silk; collage layered, stitched, cut
    Photos by Petronella Ytsma

▼ Golden Shimmer Triptych | 2008
    56 x 148 inches (1.4 x 3.7 m)
    Silk; collage layered, stitched, cut
    Photos by P. Meyer/C. Hooker

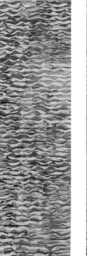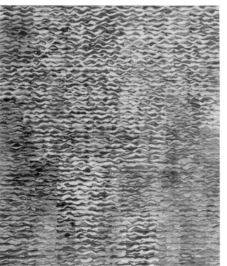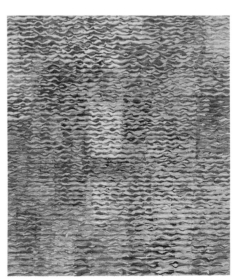

TIM HARDING

◀ **Self-Portrait Shroud** | 2009
331 x 44 inches (8.4 x 1.1 m)
Silk; collage layered, stitched, cut
Photos by Petronella Ytsma

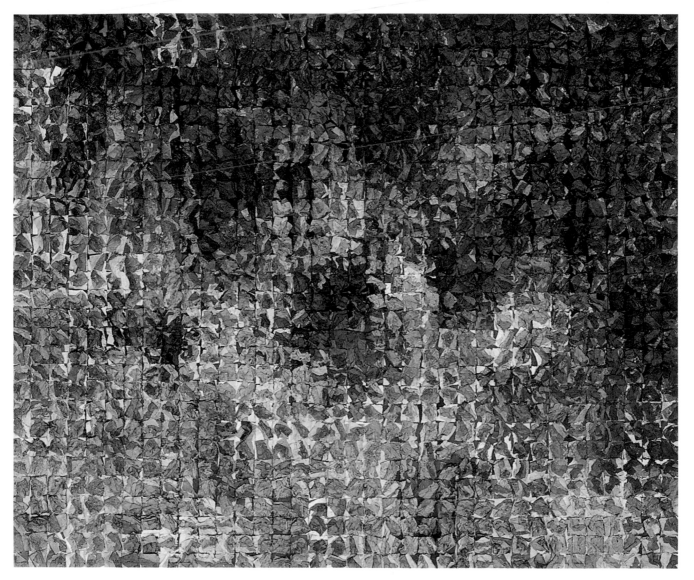

▲ **Gold Canopy Grid** | 2009

45 x 54 inches (1.1 x 1.4 m)
Silk; collage layered, stitched, cut
Photo by P. Meyer/C. Hooker

About the Curator

Martha Sielman has served since 2004 as Executive Director of Studio Art Quilt Associates, Inc. (SAQA), the world's largest art-quilt organization. A quilter since 1988, she has been involved in the arts for more than 20 years, working as a professional artist, author, lecturer, curator, juror, and arts administrator.

Sielman was curator of the book *Masters: Art Quilts, Volume 1* (Lark Crafts, 2008) and the exhibit Masters Art Quilts: 1, which traveled to the International Quilt Festivals in Houston, Chicago, and Long Beach, California, as well as to the National Quilt Museum in Paducah, Kentucky, and the New England Quilt Museum in Lowell, Massachusetts. She has written articles for *The Crafts Report* and *SAQA Journal* and appeared on the HGTV show *Simply Quilts*. Sielman served as a juror for *Pushing the Limits: New Expressions in Hooked Art*.

She has both witnessed and participated in the explosive growth of art quilting. SAQA has more than 2,700 members from more than 30 countries, and in 2010 the organization received a Visual Arts grant from the National Endowment for the Arts.

Sielman lives in Storrs, Connecticut, with her husband, five children, and two cats.

◀ I Always Wear Makeup When I Go Shopping | 2004
70 x 37 x 25 inches (1.8 x 0.9 x 0.6 m)
Folding screen, mannequin, recycled clothing, wig, lamé, hook-and-loop tape; machine appliquéd, machine quilted, assembled
Photo by Richard Bergen

Acknowledgments

Any book is a collaborative effort. In order to make this project happen, Lark Crafts employed a wonderful team of editors: Ray Hemachandra, Julie Hale, and Larry Shea. Their assistance was invaluable. Additionally, the art department at Lark produced a wonderful layout that allows readers to experience the color and texture of each beautiful quilt.

Along with the terrific folks at Lark, I would like to thank Jacquie Atkins, Caroline Couturier, Linda Colsh, Kathleen Dawson, Sylvia Einstein, Noriko Endo, Bruce Hoffman, Ryoko Kobayashi, Gul LaPorte, Mirjam Pet-Jacobs, Carolyn Mazloomi, Sandra Sider, and Jack Walsh for their help in contacting (and in some cases interpreting for) the artists whose work is presented here.

Finally, I want to thank my husband, David, and my children, Ben, Katie, Daniel, Lucy, and Jonathan, for giving me the gift of many long weekends so that I could focus on this book.

— Martha Sielman, curator

Martha Sielman is a tireless ambassador for, and champion of, art quilting. It was an enormous pleasure to reunite and work with her again, as we did on *Masters: Art Quilts, Volume 1*, the equally magnificent first volume in this series.

Martha thanked editors Julie Hale and Larry Shea, and I'll extend that thanks to Amanda Carestio, Dawn Dillingham, Gavin Young, and the entire Lark Needlearts team. Kay Holmes Stafford, who worked with me on the lovely book *500 Art Quilts*, provided layout and design, joined by Megan Kirby and cover designer Meagan Shirlen. Todd Kaderabek and Lance Wille offered their usual outstanding production support.

Speaking for all of us, I especially thank the quilters who took the time to share images of their work and thoughts about their art, allowing us to create this exceptionally beautiful book.

— Ray Hemachandra, senior editor

Portrait Photographers

We thank the photographers whose portraits of the artists appear in this book:

Geneviève Attinger, photo by Perrine Attinger
Rachel Brumer, photo by David Cohn
Maryline Collioud-Robert, photo by Aude Collioud
Jane Dunnewold, photo by Zenna James
Pamela Fitzsimons, photo by David Barnes
Karin Franzen, photo by Madera Hill
Chunghie Lee, photo by Jiyoung Chung
Linda MacDonald, photo by Bob Comings
Paula Nadelstern, photo by Marianne Barcellona
Mirjam Pet-Jacobs, photo by Robert Pet
Emily Richardson, photo by Rick Fine
Arturo Alonzo Sandoval, photo by Tim Collins
Anna Torma, photo by Nora Herting
Dirkje van der Horst-Beetsma, photo by Fred van der Horst

The photos of Izabella Baykova, Alice Beasley, Tafi Brown, Elizabeth Busch, Dorothy Caldwell, Carolyn Crump, Rosalie Dace, Daniela Dancelli, Fenella Davies, Dianne Firth, Gayle Fraas, Leslie Gabriëlse, Margery Goodall, Tim Harding, Misik Kim, Bente Vold Klausen, Beatrice Lanter, Shulamit Liss, Patricia Malarcher, Eleanor McCain, Jan Myers-Newbury, Reiko Naganuma, Risë Nagin, Duncan Slade, Jim Smoote, Nelda Warkentin, and Laura Wasilowski are self-portraits.

Index of Artists

▲ White Is White | 2008

Maryline Collioud-Robert
51³/₁₆ x 43⁵/₁₆ inches (1.3 x 1.1 m)
Cotton; machine pieced, machine appliquéd

Photo by artist